SMALL SPACE
COOKING

SMALL SPACE
COOKING

·····································

Simple, Quick, and Healthy Recipes
for the Tiny Kitchen

Hope Korenstein

Photography by
Jennifer Silverberg

Skyhorse Publishing

Table of Contents

Introduction

Winter, 2022

It's not often that we get second chances in life. I think I assumed that if I ever got a shot at a second chance, I would spring into action. Well, I was wrong. I'm sorry to report that when my second chance at doing this book came, I froze. Option paralysis immediately set in. What should I change? (Aside, obviously, from the typos.) Which recipes get the heave-ho, and which ones get their chance in the spotlight? It's been eight years since the book was published, and cooking, like life, evolves over time. When the book first hit the shelves, I was married, with a baby and a toddler. Now, I'm divorced, with a kid and a tween. Both of my kids—and I am embarrassed to admit this—are terrible eaters, who will sit glumly at the dinner table if confronted by something they do not wish to consume.

It was my picky kids who gave me the answer. The favorite recipes remained, and the recipes that had fallen out of rotation were replaced with the unicorns, the dishes that we all love, those that can be made with minimum fuss, and where the recipe is somehow greater than the sum of its parts. These new arrivals range from Zucchini Pancakes (page 106), to Buttermilk Coffee Cake (page 119), from Kung Pao Chicken (page 39) to Shrimp with Lemongrass (page 55).

And, while some things in my life have changed, others have stayed the same. I first wrote this book because I loved to cook, but to do so meant dealing with all of the physical limitations of my tiny kitchen: the absence of counter space to spread out, the lack of kitchen equipment because there was no place to store it, the desire not to dirty too many dishes because there was no dishwasher. Now, I have a slightly larger kitchen (with a dishwasher!), but, as a single mom with a full-time job, I don't have a lot of time to fuss over dinner. Small kitchen cooking is how I still cook, because it conserves space and time. These days, I have a little more of the first, but much less of the second.

This second chance also means that I get to tell you about how the original book made it to the shelves in the first place. It began with a problem: I had trouble replicating a dish that people liked, because I forgot how I had made it. So, I started writing recipes down. I drafted the book, somehow stumbled onto an agent who was willing to take on the project, and then . . . nothing happened. For, like, ten years.

Fast forward to 2012. I was living in Brooklyn, in an apartment with a marginally less tiny kitchen, on maternity leave from my job after having given birth to my second child. Out of the blue, I received a phone call that the book was going to be published. But there was a catch: it needed images. In a panic, I called Jennifer Silverberg, a brilliant photographer who also happens to be an old friend. Lucky for me, Jenn is the kind of person who is willing to go the extra mile for a friend—or, in this case, an extra 975 miles, which is the distance between her house in St. Louis and my apartment in Brooklyn. (If Jenn were here, at this point she would probably explain that, approximately one thousand years ago, when we were in college together, she was short a few credits for the upcoming semester, so I suggested she take a photography internship at the alternative weekly paper where I had a writing internship, thus helping her get her first job in the field that became her career.) Anyway, Jenn and her husband immediately made plans to come to New York. Over the course of a week, Jenn and I shot the book out of my Brooklyn apartment. My mom came too, to lend a hand with prep, wash dishes, and help take care of the baby. Jenn and her husband stayed with my parents in New Jersey, and every night I sent them back to the 'burbs with dinner, the dishes that we had cooked and photographed that day. I think the beautiful images in the book reflect what an amazing experience it was, and how special the time that the three of us (plus my baby son) spent cooking and shooting in my apartment.

I hope you enjoy the recipes in the latest edition of this book, and maybe share them with family and friends. This book never would have happened without the help of my family and friends, and what better way to show your appreciation for your loved ones than by cooking for them?

Five Tips for Cooking Great Food

Of course, there's no guarantee that everything you cook will taste great, but there are a few things you can do—especially if you haven't done much cooking—that can help you out.

1. Cook what is in season. Not only will your food taste better, but you'll also save money. When your grocer can get produce from local farmers, it costs much less than when he has to schlep it here from another country. And if it came from another country, chances are it was picked long before it's hitting your grocery cart, so it's not even very fresh.

2. Use good ingredients. This is kind of a corollary to cooking what is in season, but it's just as important. Try to use good cheeses. Buy some good quality olive oil for salads (but don't bother using the good olive oil for cooking).

3. Read the whole recipe before you start cooking. This may seem obvious, but I often find myself glancing at the ingredient list and then glazing out the rest of the recipe. If you read the entire recipe, and make sure you understand what you need to do, then there's no danger that you'll get halfway through the recipe and then get stuck.

4. Taste the dish as you cook it. This is so important! If you taste the food as you cook it, you can make sure that it will taste good when it hits the table. And if you taste it and it doesn't taste good to you, think about what might make it better. Which brings me to my next suggestion . . .

5. Use salt! One of the main reasons that a new cook's food doesn't taste good is that there isn't enough salt. If the flavors taste dull, or bland, salt can magically brighten up the dish. While I'm on the subject of salt, I should mention that I use kosher salt in all of my recipes. It is available at every grocery store. The big difference between kosher salt and table salt is the size of the salt crystals. Kosher salt has larger crystals, which are easier to pinch and measure with your fingers. I store kosher salt in an old jelly jar, so it is easy for me to grab a pinch of salt and throw it into what I am cooking. (If I tried to grab table salt, it would slide right through my fingers.)

A FEW WORDS ABOUT SERVING SIZES: I am of the opinion that leftovers in the refrigerator are like money in the bank, so I usually cook meals with a built-in plan of leftovers. Most of my recipes serve two with leftovers for lunches or another meal during the week. If you are less enamored of leftovers than I am, you can always cut recipe amounts.

Equipment List

While I'm not prepared to say that you absolutely, positively must possess the following equipment list, it will certainly make your life easier in the kitchen.

A GOOD QUALITY SHARP KNIFE: A sharp knife is a beautiful thing. Suddenly, it is easy to cut food, and it takes so much less time than fighting those vegetables with an old, dull knife. Of course, it also takes much less time to cut *yourself* so be careful!

SILICONE-TIPPED TONGS: Next to my knife, this is the tool I reach for the most when I'm cooking. I use tongs basically as an extension of my hand, for grabbing hot food, turning food over, and stirring. Make sure to buy silicone-tipped tongs, which won't scratch the pots and pans.

ONE LARGE POT: If you don't have one already, I'd like to suggest a dutch oven, rather than a pasta pot. A seven-quart dutch oven has a wider mouth than a pasta pot, which makes it easier to stir things like soups and stews. Some dutch ovens are super heavy (and expensive) but you can find cheaper, aluminum dutch ovens that are reasonably priced.

TWO PANS: A twelve-inch skillet and a ten-inch skillet should do the trick. Try to find heavy pans, because they will conduct the heat better than lighter ones and food is less likely to burn. I like non-stick skillets, but take a careful look at the pans; if it looks like the non-stick coating might come off, chances are that it will come off. And it will come off into your food—not the ideal seasoning.

A RIMMED COOKIE SHEET: This is perfect for roasting vegetables. The rim makes it easy to toss everything with your hands without the vegetables jumping overboard.

A TWO-SIDED CUTTING BOARD: Make sure you designate one side of the board for raw chicken and meat, and the other side for everything else.

A COLANDER: For draining pasta and rinsing vegetables.

A LARGE BOWL: For tossing salads and for the occasional baking project.

A BOX GRATER: For shredding cheese and grating vegetables.

A VEGETABLE PEELER: For carrots, potatoes, etc.

A ZESTER: I have to include this because I use mine all the time. It's great for grating hard cheese and taking the rind off of oranges and lemons. It is also, hands down, the best way to grate ginger.

A WOODEN SPOON: For stirring.

MEASURING CUPS: For measuring.

A POTATO MASHER: For mashing.

Salads and Starters

NO LETTUCE REQUIRED: I love greens, but a few years ago I developed an aversion to washing and drying lettuce. The result is that I created some easy salad recipes including only ingredients that are washable, dryable, and chop-able. I've since overcome the aversion (it helps that I can buy pre-washed greens when I just don't feel like pulling out the salad spinner) and so there are several salads using greens included here as well.

Vinaigrette

Makes about 1 cup

I use this on every kind of salad you can imagine, and it always tastes great. It's also incredibly easy to make. I usually throw some together on a Sunday and then use it all week. I think it tastes much better than anything you can buy in a bottle.

Ingredients:

1 teaspoon Dijon mustard
½ teaspoon honey
3 tablespoons lemon juice, cider
    vinegar, or white wine vinegar

Salt and pepper
⅔ cup good olive oil

Directions:

Mix together the mustard and honey, then add the lemon juice or vinegar. Add a big pinch of salt and a few grinds of pepper. Slowly whisk in olive oil, or shake everything together in a glass jar with a screw-top lid. That way, you can store the vinaigrette in the same container that you made it in.

NOTE: You can add garlic, thyme, cilantro or any other herb you like.

Panzanella

Serves 2

Panzanella is technically a bread salad, and you are certainly welcome to add cubes of stale bread to this recipe, but I've found that I prefer this salad with a crusty loaf of bread alongside. Add some cheese, maybe some prosciutto, and a glass of wine, and you have a great summer meal, without ever turning on the stove. Make this at the end of the summer, when the tomatoes are at their best. I don't use vinegar here—the juice from the tomatoes adds plenty of acidity.

Ingredients:

4 large, very ripe tomatoes
1 small red onion
2 Kirby or Persian cucumbers, or ½
    English cucumber
½ ball fresh mozzarella cheese

½ red pepper
Handful of basil leaves (optional)
3 tablespoons olive oil
Salt and pepper to taste
½ cup pitted olives

Directions:

Coarsely chop the tomatoes and throw them in a large bowl with some salt. Thinly slice the red onion and add that. Cut the cucumbers into thick rounds and add to the bowl (peeling is optional). Cut the cheese into cubes and add to the bowl. Cut the red pepper into thin strips, then cut each strip into thirds and add that. Tear up the basil leaves, if you are using them, and add. Dress with olive oil and season with salt and pepper. Add the olives, toss everything together, and serve.

Best Kale Salad

Serves 2, with leftovers

When it comes to kale, there are two kinds of people: the people who love kale and can't stop throwing it into their salads and smoothies, and the people who find kale incredibly annoying and think it tastes like a box of hair.

For me, kale depends on which kind you buy, and how you prepare it. This recipe—courtesy of *Bon Appetit*—features Lacinato kale (also called Tuscan kale, or Dinosaur kale) that is finely shredded. (I roll the leaves up like a cigar, and then thinly slice the leaves into ribbons.) Most salads get dressed at the last minute, so they don't get soggy. But if kale is dressed long before serving, it can absorb the vinaigrette; here, the shredded kale and brussels sprouts really soak in the mustard-lemon vinaigrette. With toasted almonds and Pecorino cheese, it is absolutely delicious.

Ingredients:

½ cup almonds
2 bunches of Tuscan kale, shredded
½ pound brussels sprouts, trimmed and grated or thinly sliced
¾ cup grated Pecorino
1 small shallot

1 clove garlic
2 tablespoons Dijon mustard
1 tsp grainy mustard
½ cup fresh lemon juice
Salt and pepper
½ cup olive oil

Directions:

In a dry pan, toast the almonds until they are fragrant and slightly darker in color, then reserve.

Mince the shallot and smash and chop the garlic. Mix together the shallot, garlic, both types of mustard, and lemon juice. Season with salt and pepper. Whisk in the olive oil until everything is well combined, then toss with the shredded kale and brussels sprouts. (I do this an hour or so before I plan on serving the salad.)

Right before serving, toss the cheese with the kale and brussels sprouts. Sprinkle the toasted almonds on top and serve.

Thai Mango Salad

Serves 4, or 2 with leftovers

This is a very refreshing, hot weather salad. As always, the hot sauce is to taste. This salad benefits from sitting around a while and tastes better the day after it has been made.

Ingredients:

Juice of 1 lime
2 teaspoons honey or sugar
1 teaspoon grated ginger
1 tablespoon fish sauce, or soy sauce,
  or even just a big pinch of salt
½ teaspoon Sriracha or any hot sauce
  you like

2 small cucumbers, like Kirby or Persian
1 small red onion
1 mango
½ small jicama
3 scallions
Bunch of mint
Bunch of cilantro

Directions:

In the bottom of a bowl large enough to hold the salad, squeeze in the lime juice, and let the honey or sugar dissolve into it. Add the ginger, fish sauce, and Sriracha, and stir together. Taste and correct for seasoning. If the dressing is too spicy, some more honey will cut the heat.

Cut the cucumbers, red onion, mango, and jicama into medium dice. Slice the scallions and chop the mint and cilantro. Dump everything into the bowl, and stir until the vegetables are coated.

ON JICAMA: Jicama is a crunchy root that has some sweetness and a little starchiness; it has been described as a cross between an apple and a potato. It is terrific in salads or served alongside dips. You can certainly leave it out here, but I think it adds a nice crunch.

Roasted Red Pepper–Feta Dip

Serves 8–10 as a starter

This dip is a terrific starter that is off the beaten path of the standard, mayonnaise-based dip, and it's incredibly easy to make. You will need to whiz everything together, but if you don't have a food processor, those mini choppers sell for very little money, don't take up much space, and are seriously handy. Or, you could finely chop everything, for a chunkier dip. I serve this with vegetables and pita chips. The horseradish gives the whole thing just the right kick. I love roasted peppers, and they are a cinch to make, but if you don't have the time or inclination, you can certainly substitute a store-bought jar.

Ingredients:

3 red bell peppers
⅓ cup feta cheese
3 tablespoons olive oil

Juice of 1 lemon
1 clove garlic, chopped
1 tablespoon prepared horseradish

Directions:

First, roast the peppers. Simply stick the whole peppers under the broiler and cook, turning, until they are black on all sides, which will take about 5 minutes per side. Put the cooked peppers in a paper bag to cool.

When the peppers are cooled, peel and seed them. Blend them with the rest of the ingredients. Taste the dip—it might need a touch of salt.

ON ROASTED PEPPERS: They are so easy to make and are terrific on sandwiches, in salads, or even tossed with some pasta and your favorite cheese. Rinse off the pepper and place it whole under the broiler. Broil until it is charred all over. (You'll have to rotate the pepper to get uniform blackness.) Remove the pepper and put it in a paper bag, to steam off the skin. When the pepper is cool, the skin should slide off the flesh, and it should be very easy to pull out the stem and seeds and to pull the pepper into strips. Place them in a jelly jar or plastic container with a pinch of salt and a splash of olive oil. They will keep for a week.

Figs with Honey Balsamic Glaze and Whipped Goat Cheese

Serves 4–6 as a starter

When fresh figs hit the markets, I always grab some. They are great all by themselves, and spectacular when you add a little bit of balsamic and cayenne-spiked honey and some whipped goat cheese. These are a snap to make, and taste great with a glass of wine or a cold drink. I've served the figs with the whipped goat cheese piled on top, but they are also tasty with the figs on top of crostini spread with goat cheese. You can also spread the whipped goat cheese on crostini and top it with all kinds of things: halved, salted grape tomatoes; roasted peppers; thin slices of radish; or smoked salmon.

Ingredients:

1 teaspoon honey
1 teaspoon best quality balsamic
  vinegar
Cayenne pepper, to taste
Salt
1 (4-oz) log of plain goat cheese, room
  temperature

1–2 teaspoons olive oil
1 tablespoon warm water (if needed)
Freshly ground pepper
1 container of fresh figs (I like the black
  Mission figs)

Directions:

In a small bowl, mix together the honey, balsamic vinegar, a generous shake of cayenne pepper, and a big pinch of salt. Taste, and make sure the level of heat is to your liking.

In a mini chopper or blender, dump the goat cheese, add several grinds of pepper and a drizzle of olive oil. Whip the ingredients together, adding in a bit of warm water if the goat cheese looks clumpy.

To serve, halve the figs, then swipe a bit of the honey mixture on each half, and top with a small spoonful of goat cheese. Or, slice up a baguette, toast the slices, and spread each slice with some whipped goat cheese, top with a couple of the honey-swiped fig halves.

Aunt Nicki's Parsley de la Maison

Serves 4–6 as a starter

My Aunt Nicki is a fantastic cook who has been feeding crowds for decades, and makes it all seem effortless. Everything she makes is great, but the little nibbles she serves with drinks are unfailingly delicious. Her love of appetizers is deep and abiding. Every day at 5:00 p.m., Aunt Nicki and my Uncle Jack—who are both in their nineties—still share Aunt Nicki's homemade starters and a glass of wine. This simple and tasty carrot-parsley combination has long been a family favorite. It takes no time to put together in a food processor or mini-chopper, and can be served with mini toasts or wedges of pita.

Ingredients:

1 very small onion
2 cloves garlic
1 large bunch of Italian parsley
2 large carrots, finely grated

¼ cup wine vinegar
½ cup olive oil
½ teaspoon salt
¼ teaspoon crushed red pepper flakes

Directions:

In a food processor or mini-chopper, whiz the onion and garlic. Add the parsley leaves and briefly process. Dump the onion-garlic-parsley mixture into a large bowl and mix in the carrots, vinegar, olive oil, salt and red pepper flakes. Taste and correct for seasoning—it might need a dash more salt.

Serve with mini toasts, crackers, pita wedges or slices of a baguette.

Gravlax

Serves 10–12 as an appetizer

This recipe is such a show-stopper, and it is so ludicrously easy to make that I had to include it. The only thing you need is time—about two days, to allow the salmon to cure. Seriously, the hardest part of this dish is slicing the salmon after it has finished curing. This is delicious served with small rye or pumpernickel rounds.

Ingredients:

⅓ cup kosher salt
⅓ cup sugar
1 tablespoon ground black pepper
2 pounds of salmon fillets
1 large bunch dill sprigs

MUSTARD SAUCE:
2 tablespoons white wine vinegar
1 tablespoon sugar
4 tablespoons Dijon mustard
⅓ cup olive oil
2 tablespoons chopped dill

Directions:

Mix together the salt, sugar, and pepper. Cut the salmon in half lengthwise. Dry the flesh with paper towels, then sprinkle it evenly with the salt-sugar mixture and rub it in slightly. Place the dill on top of one half of the salmon, then place the other salmon half, flesh side down, on top of the dill, so that you have a sort of sandwich of salmon, with the skin sides out and the dill in the middle. Put it in a dish, cover it with foil, and weigh it down with cans or bricks or whatever you have around. Put it in the refrigerator for 36 hours, flipping it every 12 hours.

Meanwhile, make the mustard dill sauce by combining the white vinegar, 1 tablespoon sugar, Dijon mustard, olive oil, and chopped dill..

When the salmon is cured, remove the dill and as much of the salt-sugar mixture as possible. Thinly slice the salmon against the grain and serve.

My Mom's Broccoli Salad

Serves 4

My mom has been making this salad for as long as I can remember, and she always receives rave reviews. This is great in the summer and can easily be doubled or tripled for a crowd.

Ingredients:

1 head broccoli
½ cup sliced black olives
6 thinly sliced radishes
6 tablespoons olive oil
3 tablespoons red wine vinegar
1 teaspoon salt

Ground black pepper
¼ teaspoon dry mustard
1 clove garlic, minced
2 tomatoes, cut into wedges
½ cup feta cheese, crumbled
2 tablespoons pine nuts, toasted

Directions:

Cut the broccoli into florets. Drop them into a pot of boiling water for one minute, to blanch them. (If you prefer, you can also leave the broccoli raw.) Dump the broccoli into a large bowl and add the olives and radishes.

Whisk together the olive oil, vinegar, salt, pepper, mustard, and garlic. Toss with the vegetables and marinate for several hours in the refrigerator.

Before serving, toss with the tomatoes, feta cheese, and pine nuts.

Baby Spinach Salad

Serves 4 as a starter salad

I love using pre-washed baby spinach in salads, partly because I'm lazy and prefer not having to wash and dry my greens, and partly because I find that baby spinach holds up better than mixed greens—although you can use any greens you like for this recipe. This salad turns out surprisingly elegant and delicious. The trick to the salad is the pecans, which add an indescribably sweet and crunchy element. If you don't care for blue cheese, you can also use feta.

Ingredients:

2 tablespoons lemon juice
Pinch of cayenne pepper
Big pinch of salt
¼ cup olive oil
4 cups baby spinach

½ red onion, thinly sliced
¼ cup crumbled blue cheese
¼ cup dried cranberries
¼ cup pecans

Directions:

In the bottom of the bowl in which you intend to serve the salad, whisk together the lemon juice, cayenne, and salt, and then slowly whisk in the olive oil. Add the spinach and red onion and toss with the dressing. Add the blue cheese and cranberries.

In a toaster oven or a dry pan on the stovetop, lightly toast the pecans. Be careful not to burn them. Distribute them over the top and serve.

SALADS AND DRESSINGS: I often whisk the dressing right into the bottom of the salad bowl, pile my salad ingredients in, and toss everything together. However, with a salad that involves greens, it will get soggy if you leave it lying around for a while dressed. If you don't plan on serving it immediately, whisk the dressing together in a separate container and toss with the salad at the last minute.

Arugula Salad with Shaved Parmesan

Serves 4 as a starter salad

Please use the absolute best Parmesan cheese you can find in this salad. It is expensive, but a little goes a long way, and the stuff will last for weeks in your fridge.

Ingredients:

1½ tablespoons white wine vinegar
4 tablespoons olive oil
Salt and pepper
4 cups arugula, or any combination of
  greens, washed and dried, with large
  stems removed

2 small tomatoes, diced
1 large or 2 small red peppers, roasted
1 hunk of Parmesan cheese

Directions:

In the bottom of the bowl in which you want to serve the salad, whisk together the white wine vinegar, olive oil, salt, and pepper.

Right before serving, toss the greens with the dressing. Scatter the tomatoes on top, and then lay some strips of roasted pepper on top. Finally, using a vegetable peeler, shave slices of Parmesan over the top and serve.

Guacamole

Makes about 3 cups

When avocados are ripe, it just doesn't get any better than this.

Ingredients:

3 ripe avocados
1 small tomato, diced (I squeeze the
   seeds out first)
⅓ cup diced red onion
1 clove garlic, smashed and minced
1–2 tablespoons lime juice

Generous handful of chopped cilantro
   (If you don't like cilantro, leave it out)
Salt
Black pepper
Pinch of cayenne pepper

Directions:

Cut the avocado in half, then twist to separate the halves. Remove the large pit in the center, then use a large spoon to scoop out the flesh. Coarsely chop the avocado, then add it to a bowl with the rest of the ingredients. Mix everything together, then taste and correct for seasoning. It might need more salt, or another squeeze of lime juice. Serve with tortilla chips.

ON AVOCADOS: When are avocados ripe? California avocados are the ones that look like they are encased in crocodile skin. The avocado is ripe when it is dark brown, and it gives ever so slightly when squeezed. Inside, the avocado should be light green, without any brown spots. There is a giant pit in the middle of the fruit, so run a knife around the circumference of the avocado, then twist the halves of the fruit and pull. Dislodge the pit, then use a big spoon to scoop out the flesh and cut it into cubes. Avocado will turn brown once it is cut, so add a bit of lemon juice or lime juice on the surface of any avocado that you are not using. You can also place plastic wrap directly on the flesh of the cut half of an avocado to store it without risk of browning.

Salsa

Makes about 2 cups of salsa

I'm not opposed to buying salsa in jars, but it's so easy to make the stuff, and it tastes fresher than anything you can buy. You can get creative with this recipe and throw in any herbs or ingredients you like. As always, use as much or as little jalapeño as you like.

Ingredients:

4 large ripe tomatoes
Pinch of salt and a few grinds of pepper
1 small red onion
1 jalapeño, minced

2 scallions
1–2 limes, juiced
Handful of cilantro, chopped (if you
    don't like cilantro, leave it out)

Directions:

Cut the tomatoes in half and squeeze out the seeds for a drier salsa, or leave the seeds for a wetter one. Dice and put them in a bowl. Sprinkle the tomatoes with salt and pepper. (It helps release the juices and make it more liquid-y and therefore salsa-y). Dice up the red onion, mince the jalapeño, and thinly slice the scallions and add to the tomatoes. Stir in the lime juice, top with cilantro if desired, and serve.

Parmesan Roasted Asparagus with Eggs

Serves 4 as a starter or 2 for brunch

This is a great first course or brunch dish, and a really easy and tasty way to make asparagus. You can also skip the eggs and just roast the asparagus to serve it as a side dish. I can eat this for dinner, along with a good piece of bread to soak up all the eggy goodness.

Ingredients:

1 bunch of asparagus
1½ tablespoons olive oil
Salt and pepper

2 tablespoons grated Parmesan cheese
  (the good stuff, please)
2 tablespoons butter
4 eggs

Directions:

Preheat oven to 400°F. Trim the woody ends off the asparagus. Put them on a cookie sheet and toss them with the olive oil, salt and pepper, and Parmesan cheese. Roast them in the oven until they are slightly brown, about 10 minutes.

While the asparagus is roasting, melt butter in a pan on low heat. Add the eggs, being careful not to break the yolks, and cook them until the whites are set and they are sunny side up, about 3 minutes.

Put the asparagus onto plates and top with the eggs. Sprinkle the eggs with salt and pepper and serve.

Chicken and Meat

NO BONES ABOUT IT: This chapter has a chicken recipe for just about everybody. I've also included a couple of pork and meat recipes that use some of the cheaper cuts available. I know that when faced with the task of cooking dinner, sometimes the prospect of dealing with bones and skin is more than a body can stand—as a result, I use only boneless and skinless cuts of meat.

Chicken (or Tofu) with Ginger Scallion Sauce

Serves 4

I probably make this dish once a week in the summer, because the sauce doesn't have to cook, and it's a snap to mix together. Simply cook the chicken and serve it with rice and the sauce. You can also easily substitute tofu for chicken to make this dish vegan.

Ingredients:

¼ cup + 1 tablespoon vegetable oil, divided
¼ cup soy sauce
⅓ cup minced scallions
2–3 tablespoons grated ginger root

1 teaspoon toasted sesame oil
1 teaspoon hot chili oil
1½ pounds chicken or tofu
1 pound of vegetables, any kind

Directions:

Mix together ¼ cup vegetable oil, soy sauce, scallions, ginger, sesame oil, and chili oil. You can make the sauce ahead of time, and it will keep for up to a week in the refrigerator.

Add the remaining tablespoon of oil to a large pan. Add the chicken and sauté until cooked through, about 5 to 10 minutes per side, depending on the thickness of the chicken. If you are using tofu, see the box below for my favorite way to cook it.

After the chicken or tofu is cooked, remove it to a plate and sauté the vegetables in the same pan; if you are using something like broccoli, it will only take 2 to 3 minutes for it to cook through.

Serve with rice on a big platter, with the sauce in a bowl on the side to spoon over everything.

> HOW TO COOK CRISPY TOFU: Cut a block of firm tofu into slices about ¾-inch thick. Cover with a towel or paper towel, and weigh down the tofu for about 30 minutes, to press out the water. Season the slices with salt. Put some cornstarch or flour on a plate and thinly dredge the tofu slices on both sides. Heat vegetable oil in a pan large enough to comfortably fit all of the tofu slices, then sauté until the tofu changes color slightly and gets crispy on the outside, about 5 minutes per side. If you're feeling fancy, sprinkle a few drops of toasted sesame oil into the pan right before the tofu is finished, sprinkle with salt, and serve immediately.

White Beans with Sausage and Swiss Chard

Serves 2, with generous leftovers

This dish—maybe it's a stew, but I'm not sure—comes together in a snap, but the results are soulful and satisfying. I start with uncooked chicken sausage, but you can use whatever kind of sausage you like. Don't forget the shot of balsamic vinegar at the end! That, plus a Parmesan cheese, gives the dish a deep flavor and velvety texture.

Ingredients:

2 tablespoons olive oil
1 onion, chopped
1 teaspoon fresh thyme
3–4 cloves garlic, smashed and minced
1½ pounds sausage
1½ tablespoons tomato paste
2 (15-oz) cans white beans, drained
3 cups chicken stock

1 Parmesan rind (only if you have one lying around)
1 large bunch of swiss chard, cleaned, stemmed, and coarsely chopped
1–2 tablespoons best quality balsamic vinegar
Freshly grated Parmesan cheese.

Directions:

Heat oil in a large pot over medium heat. Add the onion and cook until it is soft, about 5 minutes, then add the thyme and garlic, and cook just until the garlic is fragrant.

Remove the sausage from its casing and add it to the pot, breaking it up with a wooden spoon as it cooks. When the sausage is brown, push everything in the pot to one side, and create an open spot. Add a splash more olive oil to the open spot, then add the tomato paste to the oil. Cook until the tomato paste is slightly darker in color. Mix it in with the vegetables and sausage, then add the white beans, together with the chicken stock. If you have a Parmesan rind, toss it in, then lower the heat, cover the pot, and simmer for about 10 minutes.

Add the swiss chard and cook until it wilts a bit. Add the balsamic vinegar, give everything one last stir, and serve, topping each bowl with freshly grated Parmesan cheese.

PARMESAN RINDS: If you buy fresh Parmesan cheese, don't throw out the rind after you've eaten all of the cheese. The rind—which lasts a long time in the freezer—adds great flavor to soups and stews.

Cornmeal-Crusted Chicken with Arugula Salad

Serves 2, with leftovers

In this recipe, the cornmeal is a quick way to give the chicken a bit of a crispy crust. The brown sugar and cayenne pepper give the chicken a sweet-spicy flavor, which works really well with the pepperiness of the arugula and the buttery-ness of the avocado. As always, the cayenne pepper is to taste, and you can use whatever greens you like.

Ingredients:

1½ pounds chicken breasts	2 medium tomatoes
1 cup cornmeal	1 small red onion
1½ tablespoons brown sugar	½ avocado
¼ teaspoon cayenne pepper, or to taste	1 large bunch of arugula
	2 tablespoons lemon juice
Salt	Salt and pepper
3 tablespoons olive oil	4 tablespoons olive oil

Directions:

Butterfly the chicken breasts and pound until they are flat and of uniform thickness.

Heat the olive oil in a pan on medium high heat. Combine the cornmeal, brown sugar, cayenne pepper, and a big pinch of salt on a plate. Dredge the chicken breasts in the cornmeal mixture and sauté until golden on each side, about 5 minutes per side. (You might need to cook the chicken in batches.)

Squeeze the seeds out of the tomatoes and chop them. Chop the red onion and dice the avocado. Coarsely chop the arugula, and combine all of the vegetables. In a small bowl or jelly jar, squeeze the juice of the lemon, add a generous pinch of salt and pepper, then whisk in the olive oil. Dress the salad lightly, then set the chicken breasts on top of the salad and serve.

> THE BUTTERFLY EFFECT: To butterfly a chicken breast, cut it in half, width-wise, then spread open the halves like you are opening up a book. Then you can pound the chicken pieces until they are thin and of uniform thickness, which helps them cook quickly and evenly.

Chicken with Mango Salsa and Coconut Rice

Serves 2, with leftovers

This is a terrific dish, but it tastes the best in spring and summer, when mangos are ripe. The shredded coconut is optional; if you do use it, be careful to use unsweetened coconut.

Ingredients:

1 cup jasmine rice
Salt
1 cup coconut milk (light coconut milk works fine)
3 tablespoons unsweetened shredded coconut (optional)
1½ tablespoons soy sauce
2 limes, juiced, divided (about 2 tablespoons)
1 tablespoon honey
Tabasco sauce, to taste

1½ tablespoons olive oil
1½ pounds chicken breasts
2 mangos (I like the yellow champagne mangos)
1 small red onion
1 small red pepper
½ small clove garlic, finely chopped
1 jalapeño, chopped (optional for those who like heat)
Bunch of cilantro, chopped

Directions:

Put one cup of rice in a pot with some salt, one cup of water, and one cup of coconut milk. Follow the instructions for cooking the rice; generally it takes 20 minutes to have perfect rice.

Toast the shredded coconut in a dry pan until golden brown, about 3 minutes, and mix with the cooked rice.

Mix the soy sauce, juice of one lime, honey, Tabasco, and olive oil in a plastic bag, and let the chicken marinate in it for 20 minutes to 1 hour.

Chop the mangos, red onion, and red pepper and mix together in a bowl. Add the garlic and the juice of the other lime. If you are using jalapeño, add that as well. Add the chopped cilantro and mix well.

Remove the chicken from the marinade and broil it under a hot broiler until it is brown on top and just cooked through, about 8 to 12 minutes per side (depending on the thickness of the chicken). Top with the mango salsa, and serve with coconut rice.

Chicken Piccata

Serves 2, with leftovers

If I have some chicken in the refrigerator and I can't decide what to do with it, this is usually what I do. You can skip pounding the chicken, but I find that it cooks more evenly that way. Serve it with pasta or potatoes.

Ingredients:

1½ pounds chicken breasts
1 cup flour
Salt and pepper
2 tablespoons olive oil
3 tablespoons butter, divided

½ cup white wine
½ cup chicken stock (canned is fine)
1 lemon
1½ tablespoons capers
Handful of flat leaf parsley, chopped

Directions:

Butterfly the chicken breasts, then pound until they are flat and of uniform thickness. Place the flour on a plate. Dredge each chicken breast in the flour mixture. Season the chicken on both sides with salt and pepper.

Heat the oil and a tablespoon of the butter in a pan until hot. Brown the chicken on both sides in the hot pan, about 6 minutes per side, and remove it to a plate. Cover the chicken with foil to keep it warm.

After the chicken is removed from the pan, reduce the heat to low. Pour in the white wine, using a wooden spoon to scrape up the bits from the bottom of the pan. Add the chicken stock, together with the juice of the lemon and the capers. Simmer for a couple minutes, until the sauce thickens and reduces a bit. Throw in the rest of the butter and stir together the sauce. Put the chicken back in, throw the parsley on top, and serve.

Mustard-Soy Glazed Chicken

Serves 2, with leftovers

Here is another quick and easy chicken dish that I make all the time. As a bonus, nearly all of the components (except the chicken, of course) keep in the pantry. I let the chicken marinate all day, or even overnight, and the flavor is great.

Ingredients:

2 tablespoons Dijon mustard
2 tablespoons soy sauce
2 tablespoons olive oil

2 cloves garlic, finely minced
Salt and pepper to taste
1½ pounds chicken

Directions:

Mix together all the ingredients except the chicken in a plastic bag. Reserve a few spoonfuls of the mustard mixture. Add the chicken to the remainder of the mustard mixture and marinate anywhere from 10 minutes to a day.

You can either broil the chicken or grill it in a grill pan. It takes about 8 to 12 minutes per side to broil the chicken. Serve topped with a little of the reserved mustard, along with salad and a baguette.

ON BROILERS: If you are nervous to use your broiler it is helpful to consider that a broiler is basically an upside-down grill, with the heat source above the food, rather than below it. Which is why it makes such a good substitute, if you don't happen to have a barbecue. I usually broil the food about 6 inches from the heat source, so my broiling times are based on that distance. I also have the option of broiling under high or low heat, and I usually broil chicken on low heat. You may have to adjust the cooking times based on the broiler that you have. If it takes longer for the food to cook (or you accidentally burn something), don't give up! You'll get the hang of it.

Blackened Chili-Lime Chicken

Serves 2, with leftovers

This recipe is fast and so tasty. Make sure you use ancho chili powder, which is fruitier than other chilies. As always, the cayenne is to taste, and if you find you made yours too spicy, you can add a little more sugar to balance things out; if the flavors don't pop, you can add a little more salt. Please don't forget to finish off the dish with a squeeze of lime juice—it makes a big difference.

Ingredients:

3 teaspoons ancho chili powder
2 teaspoons garlic powder
1½ teaspoons Mexican oregano (or whatever oregano you have on hand)
2 teaspoons coriander
1 teaspoon cayenne pepper

2 teaspoon lime zest
2–3 teaspoons salt
2 teaspoons brown sugar
1½ pounds chicken breasts
2 tablespoons vegetable oil
Lime juice

Directions:

Mix together all of the dry ingredients. Taste and correct for seasoning until the flavors are to your spice level, salt level, and taste.

Butterfly the chicken breasts, pound until they are of uniform thickness, then pat the chicken dry with paper towels.

Heat oil in a cast iron skillet (or a large pan) over medium-high heat. Dredge each piece of chicken in the spice mixture, coating the chicken evenly, and then gently shake off the excess. Blacken the chicken in the pan until the chicken is cooked through. (It should only take a few minutes per side.)

Remove chicken to a platter, squeeze with lime, and serve.

Zen Roast Chicken (with or without Gravy)

Serves 4

When it comes to roast chicken, I've tried everything. I've rubbed a cut lemon on the skin, stuffed butter and herbs under the skin, and shoved onions and garlic into the chicken cavity. I've roasted it right side up, upside down, and at all different temperatures. I've dutifully basted the bird. No matter what, my results were always . . . good. But I was never able to achieve crackly skin, or ethereal juiciness and flavor. After trying everything, I tried nothing. And the results were amazing! I'm not even joking when I tell you that the way to make the absolute best roast chicken is to clear a large-ish space in your refrigerator and make sure your oven is clean.

Ingredients:

1 whole chicken, about 3–4 pounds
1 tablespoon salt
1 tablespoon flour

1 cup chicken stock (canned is fine)
1 tablespoon butter
Salt and pepper to taste

Directions:

A couple days before, buy the best quality whole chicken you can afford, preferably pre-trussed. Pat the chicken dry with paper towels, put it on a rack over a plate, and blizzard the top with salt. Stick the chicken, uncovered, in your refrigerator for a day or two. This will help dry out the skin, and dry-brine the flesh. You'll actually see the skin tighten on the flesh, and turn a bit pink.

An hour before you want to eat, pre-heat the oven to 450°F, and stick the chicken in the oven without doing anything else to it. I roast mine in a cast iron skillet, but you can use whatever you have handy. After that, leave it alone! No basting or messing around with it. Cook the chicken until it reaches an internal temperature of 165°F and the juices run clear, which should take about 50-60 minutes. This is where the clean oven comes in: the high temperature can create some smoke. It's a small price to pay for chicken nirvana.

Let the chicken rest for about 10 minutes before carving it. If you feel like it, now is the time to make gravy. This is optional—sometimes I just bring everything to the table, and then we all drag the chicken through the shmaltzy drippings at the bottom of the skillet before eating it, like the heathens we are. (Don't knock it until you try it; it's delicious.)

To make the gravy, pour off all but two tablespoons of fat from the pan. Over medium-low heat, add the flour, and whisk it into the fat. When the flour is integrated, add the chicken stock and whisk until the gravy is slightly thickened and reduced by about half. Whisk in the butter, add salt and pepper to taste, and serve.

Kung Pao Chicken

Serves 2, with fewer leftovers than you think you should have

If you want to know what we eat for dinner, pretty much every week, here you go. This stir fry is better than takeout, and comes together in the time it takes to cook rice. There are two secrets; the first is in using Chinese dark vinegar and dark soy sauce. The dish will survive with regular soy sauce and rice vinegar, but using the dark soy and vinegar really makes it special. The other secret is marinating the chicken in egg white, sherry, and cornstarch, which makes the chicken incredibly tender.

Ingredients:

1½ pounds chicken, sliced
1 egg white
2 teaspoons cornstarch
1 teaspoon dry sherry
2 tablespoons dark soy sauce
2 teaspoons brown sugar
2 tablespoons Chinese dark vinegar
1 teaspoon sesame oil
1 teaspoon fresh grated ginger

½ cup chicken stock or water
2 tablespoons vegetable oil
3–4 cloves garlic, chopped
3–6 dried chilies
1–2 cups broccoli (or any other vegetable you like)
1 handful peanuts
1 bunch of scallions, thinly sliced

Directions:

Slice chicken, and add the egg white, cornstarch, and dry sherry. Marinate for a few hours or overnight.

For the sauce, mix together the dark soy sauce, brown sugar, dark vinegar, sesame oil, grated ginger, and chicken stock, and set aside.

Heat the vegetable oil in a wok or large pan over medium high heat, until the oil is hot and shimmering. Stir fry the chopped garlic and dried chilies for 30 seconds, just until the garlic is fragrant. Add the broccoli and peanuts, and stir fry for another minute or two. Add the chicken, and cook for a few minutes, until the chicken barely looks cooked through. Pour in the sauce and simmer until it thickens, about two or three minutes.

Sprinkle with scallions and serve over rice.

Pork Tenderloin with Mustard-Apricot Glaze

Serves 2, with leftovers

This one is a crowd pleaser. The apricot jam gives the whole dish a little twist of sweet and fruit that goes great with the pork and the mustard.

Ingredients:

2 pounds pork tenderloin
Salt and pepper
2 tablespoons peanut oil
2 tablespoons mustard
3 tablespoons soy sauce

2 tablespoons rice vinegar
1 tablespoon apricot jam
1 clove garlic, chopped
Hot red pepper flakes

Directions:

Preheat oven to 400°F.

Season the pork tenderloin all around with salt and pepper. Heat peanut oil in a pan until hot, and sear the tenderloin on the stovetop until all sides are brown. Roast in the oven until the pork is medium rare (when a meat thermometer reads 145°F), about 10 to 15 minutes.

To make the glaze, whisk together the mustard, soy, rice vinegar, apricot jam, garlic, and hot pepper in a bowl. Spoon the glaze over the top and sides of the tenderloin while it is still hot. Let the meat rest for 10 minutes before slicing and serving.

Asian Marinated Flank Steak

Serves 2, with leftovers

I like to throw a flank steak into the marinade in the morning before work, and then broil it when I get home, but you definitely don't need to marinate it for twelve hours for the meat to taste great. You will get great flavor from marinating in as little as 20 minutes.

Ingredients:

1½ pounds flank steak
2 cloves garlic, chopped
3 scallions, white and green parts sliced
¼ cup soy sauce

2 tablespoons rice vinegar
1 tablespoon sesame oil
Several shakes of Tabasco, or any other hot sauce

Directions:

In a small bowl, mix together all of the ingredients except the steak. Line a roasting pan with aluminum foil, add the steak, and pour about half the soy mixture over the steak, turning to coat. (Reserve the other half of the sauce for serving.) Let marinate for anywhere between 20 minutes and 12 hours.

Broil the steak until medium rare, about 8 to 10 minutes per side. Let the steak rest for about 10 minutes before slicing it thin, against the grain. Serve over rice, if you like, with the reserved sauce

Beef Tenderloin with Horseradish Sauce

Serves 2 with leftovers (if you're lucky)

Tenderloin is normally quite expensive, but when it's on sale at my grocery store I snap it up. This recipe is ridiculously easy, and the results are awesome. The raw steak freezes well, too, so you can buy it on sale, and then defrost it to really impress dinner guests.

Ingredients:

1–1½ pounds beef tenderloin, trimmed and tied
1 tablespoon olive oil
Salt and pepper

FOR THE HORSERADISH SAUCE:
3 tablespoons sour cream
1 tablespoon mayonnaise
1 tablespoon Dijon mustard
1 tablespoon prepared horseradish (or more, to taste)
1 tablespoon lemon juice
1 tablespoon chopped chives
Salt and pepper

Directions:

Preheat the oven to 300°F. Allow the meat to come to room temperature, and then pat it dry with paper towels. Rub the olive oil on all sides of the meat, and then season all sides of the meat with salt and pepper. (Be generous with the seasoning.)

Heat an oven-proof pan on high heat, and then add the meat. Sear it on all sides until it is brown. (This should take about 5 minutes per side.) Put the pan in the oven and slow roast it for about 45 minutes to an hour, until it has an internal temperature of 135°F for medium rare. Allow the meat to rest for at least 10 minutes.

Meanwhile, make the horseradish sauce by mixing all the ingredients together.

Slice the steak and serve with the horseradish sauce on the side.

Aunt Bobbi's Brisket

Serves 4–6, with leftovers

As a kid, I always looked forward to going to my Aunt Bobbi's house for holidays, especially when I knew she was making brisket. It never occurred to me that I might be able to replicate it; in my mind, her talents in the brisket department had almost mythical status. So, it was something of a shock when I asked for the recipe, and learned that it's really easy to make. I also learned that she had gotten the recipe from her Aunt (my Great Aunt) Sylvia, so it feels a bit like the passing of the torch. I've changed a couple of things about it—Aunt Bobbi uses Rao's tomato sauce and adds paprika, whereas I use tomato juice and always forget paprika. It's delicious either way. It turns out that all you need to make great brisket, really, is time, which makes this dish perfect for a lazy winter weekend.

Ingredients:

1 brisket (about 5 pounds)
3–4 onions
½ pound mushrooms
1 bunch carrots
2 bay leaves

1 large (64-oz) can tomato juice or jar of
   tomato sauce
½ bottle red wine
Salt and pepper

Directions:

Preheat the oven to 350°F.

Thickly slice the onions, mushrooms, and carrots into big chunks, and place them in the bottom of a roasting pan, together with the bay leaves. Pat the brisket dry, season it generously with salt and pepper, then place it in the roasting pan. Pour in equal parts tomato juice (or tomato sauce) and red wine, until the meat is just covered with liquid. You may not use the entire can of tomato juice or sauce.

Cover the top of the pan with foil, then roast for about two hours. Remove the brisket while it is still a little hard, and slice it. Strain out the onions, mushrooms, and carrots, and return the brisket to the oven for another hour or so, until the meat is fork tender.

Remove bay leaves. Serve brisket with the reserved vegetables, with the gravy from the pan on the side. It freezes really well, and tastes better the next day.

Fish and Seafood

AT SEA: Afraid of buying mussels? Terrified of hidden salmon bones? Don't be. Fish fillets like salmon and cod can be pretty inexpensive, and if you buy the fillet, rest assured that the bones have been removed. (You can also press your fingers along the flesh of the fish: you will feel any bones that are left.) And if you're not aware of this already, cultivated mussels cost only a couple of dollars per pound. Even better, since they are cultivated they don't have long, scary beards or require much cleaning beyond a rinse under cold water.

Salmon with Bread Crumb–Dill Crust

Serves 2

Salmon, lemon, and dill go really well together. Serve with a nice salad and a good hunk of bread. As a bonus, this dish looks really nice coming out of the oven, and you can easily impress a crowd

Ingredients:

3 tablespoons fresh dill, chopped
1 tablespoon lemon zest (the skin of the lemon removed with a grater)
1 cup bread crumbs (preferably fresh, but can use panko in a pinch)

Salt and pepper
1–2 tablespoons lemon juice
2–3 tablespoons olive oil
1 tablespoon Dijon mustard
1 pound salmon

Directions:

Preheat the oven to 375°F. Toss together the chopped dill, lemon zest, bread crumbs, and salt and pepper. Mix the olive oil into the bread crumb mixture until everything is moist. Smear the mustard over the flesh of the salmon, sprinkle lemon juice over the mustard coating and then pack the bread crumb mixture on top.

Bake the salmon until it is medium rare, about 15 to 25 minutes, depending on the thickness of the salmon.

My Mom's Salmon

Serves 2

This is another of my mom's recipes. She has often served crowds with this dish, and people love it, never realizing how easy it is.

Ingredients:

⅓ cup soy sauce
3 scallions, sliced
1 tablespoon grated ginger

2 cloves garlic, chopped
1 pound salmon
1 teaspoon sugar

Directions:

Combine the soy sauce, scallions, ginger, and garlic in a plastic bag. Add the salmon and let it marinate for as much time as you have. When you are ready to cook, remove the fish from the marinade and broil the fish until it is cooked through and the top is mahogany in color, about 10 to 15 minutes, depending on the thickness of the salmon. Meanwhile, pour the sauce into a small pot, add the sugar, and boil until the sauce is somewhat thickened and reduced, 5 to 10 minutes. Pour the sauce over the salmon and serve.

ON GINGER: Ginger is such a delicious flavor, simultaneously spicy and sweet. Its texture, however, is less worthy of rapture because ginger, especially older ginger root, is very fibrous. Look for ginger root where the skin is tight and unwrinkled. Peel the skin with a small spoon, and then grate the flesh as finely as possible to get all the flavor, without the fiber.

Shrimp with Lemongrass

Serves 2

The key to this quick and tasty dish is having a microplane grater. Lemongrass—a pale green stalk that you can find in most grocery stores and Asian markets—is delicious, but the fibers are coarse. (I once used sliced lemongrass in a dish; it had the texture of toenails). But, if you use a microplane to finely grate lemongrass, the result is a cloud of flavor. (And aroma, it smells wonderful). I played around a lot with this dish, and, as it turns out, the easiest way to prepare it also happens to be the best. Throw the sauce ingredients in with the shrimp and let everything marinate for a while. After a few minutes in a hot pan, the shrimp is cooked, and the addition of a few tablespoons of water in the last minute or two of cooking creates a delicious sauce. To make a complete meal, you can throw in a handful of vegetables with the shrimp, and it's always tasty over rice.

Ingredients:

1 pound shrimp, peeled and deveined
2–3 tablespoons grated lemongrass
1–2 tablespoons grated ginger
3 cloves garlic, smashed and minced
1 small shallot, minced
1½ tablespoons fresh lime juice
1 teaspoon sugar
1 teaspoon fish sauce
Salt
2 tablespoons + 2 teaspoons of
   vegetable oil, divided
3 tablespoons chopped cilantro
   (optional)

Directions:

Pat the shrimp dry, then mix in everything but the 2 tablespoons of vegetable oil and the cilantro. Marinate the shrimp for several hours, or overnight.

In a large pan, heat the remaining vegetable oil on medium-high until it is shimmering. Dump the shrimp and the marinade into the pan. After a couple of minutes, the pan will start to look a bit dry; add a few tablespoons of water, which will pick up the brown bits from the pan and form a sauce. Cook until the shrimp are pink, about 5 minutes. Garnish with cilantro, and serve over rice.

Mussels in White Wine

Serves 4 as an appetizer, 2 as a main dish

I love this dish. You might never order mussels in a restaurant again. . . .

Ingredients:

2 tablespoons olive oil
3 cloves garlic, chopped
1 shallot, chopped
Red pepper flakes
1½ pounds mussels, scrubbed

Salt
1 cup white wine
2 tablespoons butter
Handful of flat leaf Italian parsley,
    chopped

Directions:

Heat olive oil in a pan large enough to hold the mussels. Add garlic, shallot, and red pepper flakes, and sauté on low heat until soft, about 2 to 4 minutes. (Don't burn the garlic.) Add the mussels, season with salt, then pour in the cup of wine and close the lid. Cook until the mussels open, about 5 to 10 minutes. Add the butter and shake the pan around to distribute it as it melts. Sprinkle the parsley over the top and serve with lots of bread for dunking.

Mussels Marinara

Serves 2

This is a classic recipe, and the best part is that it's so easy to make. If you buy tubes of tomato paste and anchovy paste, they will keep for quite a while in your refrigerator. The only part of this recipe that you can't store is the mussels.

Ingredients:

2 tablespoons olive oil
4 cloves garlic, chopped
1 tablespoon anchovy paste
½ teaspoon red pepper flakes
1 tablespoon tomato paste

¾ cup white wine
1 (28-oz) can crushed tomatoes
½ pound pasta
1½ pounds mussels, scrubbed
Flat leaf Italian parsley, chopped

Directions:

Add the olive oil to a large pan under medium-low heat. Add the garlic, along with the anchovy paste and red pepper flakes. Cook until the ingredients melt together, about 3 minutes. Add the tomato paste and cook until you can smell the tomato and it slightly darkens in color, about another 3 minutes. Add the wine and cook for 2 minutes. Add the tomatoes, bring to a boil, and simmer on low heat for 15 minutes.

Cook the pasta. Five minutes before the pasta is done, throw the mussels into the sauce and put the lid back on the pan. After the pasta is drained, put it in a bowl, put the sauce over the pasta, sprinkle with the parsley, and serve.

Baked Garlic Shrimp

Serves 2

I used to make garlic shrimp on the stovetop, and I invariably spent the entire time babysitting the dish, worried that the garlic would burn or the shrimp would overcook. Then I realized that if I gently cooked the garlic in some (okay, a lot) of butter, and baked everything together in the oven, the garlic will never burn and the shrimp will always be perfectly cooked. Just make sure you have plenty of bread to soak up all the delectable sauce.

Ingredients:

6 tablespoons butter
3 cloves garlic, chopped
½ teaspoon red pepper flakes
3 tablespoons white wine

1 pound shrimp, peeled and deveined
Salt and pepper
Flat leaf Italian parsley, chopped
Lemon wedges

Directions:

Preheat oven to 350°F.

In a small pot, gently heat the butter together with the garlic and red pepper flakes. When the garlic becomes fragrant, add some salt, along with the white wine, and stir until everything is combined.

Meanwhile, arrange the shrimp in a single layer in a baking dish, and season with salt and pepper. Pour the butter mixture over the shrimp, and bake in the oven until the shrimp are just cooked, 10 to 12 minutes.

Garnish with chopped parsley and lemon wedges and serve.

ON SHRIMP: I hate deveining shrimp and I'm too cheap to buy shrimp already deveined. But when you're considering the size shrimp you want to buy, remember that the bigger the shrimp, the fewer there will be per pound, and the fewer, therefore, that you will have to devein.

Fish with Gremolata

Serves 2

This one is barely even a recipe, but it's a great way to serve fish. Gremolata is a classic mixture of garlic, lemon, and parsley and is typically served with beef, but I love it with fish. Any firm, white fleshed fish will work well with this recipe. Gremolata is really nothing but a solid flavor punch, so a little goes a long way. . . .

Ingredients:

1½ teaspoons lemon zest
¼ cup parsley, chopped
3 cloves garlic, finely minced
1–2 tablespoons lemon juice

4 tablespoons olive oil, divided
Salt and pepper
1 pound of thick, white fish fillets
 (like cod)

Directions:

Preheat the oven to 375°F. Mix the lemon zest with the parsley, garlic, lemon juice, and 3 tablespoons of olive oil. Season with salt and pepper.

Season the fish with salt and pepper, and juice the other half of the lemon over the fish fillets. Drizzle with a bit of the remaining olive oil. Roast the fish in the oven until cooked through, about 12 to 18 minutes, depending on the thickness of the fish. (You can also cook the fish in a pan on the stove, or under a broiler.) Top with the gremolata and serve.

Mexican Spicy Shrimp

Serves 2

This yummy shrimp dish is light, yet spicy and substantial. Don't be put off by the number of ingredients—but if you feel overwhelmed, you can cheat by substituting store-bought salsa for the tomatoes, onions, and spices. Serve with rice.

Ingredients:

3 tablespoons olive oil
2 cloves garlic, chopped
1 jalapeño, chopped (or to taste)
½ teaspoon coriander
½ teaspoon chili powder
1 medium yellow onion, chopped
1½ pounds tomatoes, chopped

½ teaspoon oregano
1 teaspoon salt
1–2 tablespoons lime juice
1 pound shrimp, peeled and deveined
3 scallions, sliced
Handful of cilantro, chopped

Directions:

Heat the olive oil in a skillet over medium heat. Add the garlic, jalapeño, coriander, chili powder, and oregano and cook until fragrant, about 1 to 2 minutes. Add the onions and sauté until they are soft, about 5 minutes.

Add the tomatoes, the salt and the lime juice and cook until the tomatoes are very soft, about 10 to 15 minutes. If the sauce looks too dry, add some water. Add the shrimp, cover the pan, and cook for 3 to 5 minutes, until the shrimp are pink.

When the shrimp are cooked, sprinkle the scallion and cilantro over the shrimp. Serve over rice.

Old Bay Fish with Cucumber Dill Sauce

Serves 2 with leftovers

I like to use cod for this recipe, but you can really use any fish that looks good or is on sale. The cucumber dill sauce is delicious with the spicy fish, but it's also great as a dip.

Ingredients:

½ small English cucumber
⅓ cup plain yogurt (use the thick Greek yogurt)
1 tablespoon dill, finely chopped
1 tablespoon scallions, finely chopped
Salt and pepper to taste
¾ cup fresh bread crumbs or panko
2½ tablespoons Old Bay seasoning

½ teaspoon garlic powder
Salt
½ teaspoon cayenne pepper (optional, if you want more spice than from the Old Bay)
1 pound thick fish fillets, like cod
¾ cup buttermilk
2 tablespoons oil

Directions:

Preheat the oven to 375°F. To make the sauce, peel the cucumber, then slice it in half lengthwise. Use a small spoon to scoop out the seeds. Finely grate the cucumber halves on a box grater, then squeeze out as much water as you can. You should wind up with about ¼ cup of cucumber. Put the cucumber in a bowl and season with some salt. Then mix in the yogurt, dill, and scallions. Add some salt and pepper to taste.

Mix together the bread crumbs or panko with the Old Bay, garlic powder, salt, and cayenne (if you are using it). Dip the fish in the buttermilk until it is coated, then dredge the fish in the bread crumb mixture. Drizzle the oil into an oven safe dish, then place the breadcrumb-coated fish in the dish and bake until the fish is cooked through and the bread crumbs are browned, about 12 to 18 minutes.

Serve the fish with a dollop of sauce on top, and more on the side.

Pasta

PASTA: I love pasta. Who doesn't? But even when you're scrambling to put dinner on the table, there's no reason to reach for the jar of sauce. This chapter includes lots of delicious sauces that go way beyond a simple marinara. Give them a try—you may find some tasty and easy alternatives to what you find in a bottle.

Pasta Carbonara Plus

Serves 2

I've always loved pasta carbonara, which is basically pasta with bacon and eggs, but I thought that there was probably a way to lighten it up a little and actually make the dish better. Here's what I came up with. I kept all the yummy ingredients, but I've added spinach and tomatoes, to make it a one-dish supper.

Ingredients:

5 slices of bacon, chopped
1 yellow onion, finely chopped
Large handful of grape tomatoes, halved
Salt
Lots of freshly ground black pepper
½ pound long pasta like linguine

1 cup pasta cooking water
1 (10-oz) package baby spinach, coarsely chopped
2 eggs
½ cup freshly grated best-quality Parmesan cheese

Directions:

Cook the pasta, reserving 1 cup of the pasta cooking water.

In a large pan, cook the bacon over medium high heat. When the bacon is crisp, drain all but one tablespoon of the fat, add the onion, and lower the heat. Cook until the onion starts to soften and look translucent, about 3 to 5 minutes. Add the tomatoes, along with some salt and pepper. Turn the heat to low.

Toss the cooked pasta and the spinach into the pan with the bacon, onion, and tomato and toss with tongs until coated. Take the pan off the heat, crack in both eggs and toss. (If it's dry, add a little of the pasta water.) Lastly, toss in the cheese and some more pepper and serve.

Spicy Shrimp with Linguine

Serves 2, with leftovers

As the title of the recipe suggests, this recipe is for fellow chili lovers. It calls for cherry peppers, which are packed in vinegar and deliver a little acidic kick, along with some heat. Once the shrimp are peeled and deveined (an admittedly annoying task), you can make the sauce in the time it takes for the pasta to cook.

Ingredients:

¾ pound linguine
4 tablespoons olive oil, divided
1 pound shrimp, peeled and deveined
Salt and pepper
3–5 cherry peppers, sliced
1 red pepper, sliced

5–6 cloves garlic, chopped
½ cup white wine
1 tablespoon tomato paste
¼–½ cup pasta cooking water
3 tablespoons cream
½ cup chopped parsley

Directions:

Cook the pasta, reserving 1 cup of the pasta cooking water.

Heat a large skillet over medium high heat. Add 2 tablespoons of olive oil, and then add the shrimp in a single layer. Season with salt and pepper, and sauté the shrimp until they are just pink, 2 to 3 minutes per side. Remove the shrimp to a plate and cover with foil to keep warm.

Reduce the heat to low and add the rest of the olive oil. Add the cherry peppers, red pepper, and garlic. Sauté until fragrant, about 2 minutes, then add wine and tomato paste. Simmer for 3 to 5 minutes. If the sauce gets too dry, add a splash of the pasta cooking water. Add the cream, season with salt and pepper, toss the shrimp back in, and add the pasta. Toss everything together for 1 to 2 minutes, sprinkle with parsley, and serve.

Tortellini with Eggplant Puree

Serves 4, with extra sauce

This one is for any eggplant lovers out there. This sauce is pureed, which you can do using a food processor or a blender. I like this best with cheese tortellini. This sauce also freezes really well.

Ingredients:

2½ cups eggplant, peeled and diced
2 cloves garlic
1 onion
Olive oil for the pan
Salt and pepper

⅓ cup grated best-quality Parmesan
1 handful basil leaves
1–1½ cups water
1 (8-oz) can tomato sauce
1½ pounds tortellini

Directions:

Peel the eggplant, and cut into cubes. Slice the garlic. Cut the onion into a rough chop. Put some olive oil in the bottom of the skillet, and sauté the eggplant, garlic, and onion with a pinch of salt until the vegetables are soft, about 10 minutes. Let the vegetables cool slightly.

Dump the vegetables, the Parmesan, and the basil leaves in the bowl of a food processor or blender. (If you use a blender you might need to do it in batches.) Run the machine and puree, adding some water to get it to a sauce-like consistency. (This will take approximately 1 cup of water, depending on how thick you want the sauce.) Dump it back into the pan, add the can of tomato sauce, and warm it through.

Cook the tortellini. Once it is al dente, toss the tortellini with some of the sauce and serve.

Pasta with Brown Butter Mushrooms

Serves 4 as a side dish or 2 as a main course

This can be a side dish or, with a salad, a meal unto itself. Please don't leave out the dried mushrooms! Although they can be expensive, they add tons of flavor, and a little goes a long way. This dish is nice with a mix of wild mushrooms, but you can use whatever mushrooms you like.

Ingredients:

¾ pound pasta of your choice
1 ounce dried mushrooms
1 pound fresh mushrooms
6 tablespoons butter

5 cloves garlic, thinly sliced
1–2 tablespoons sherry vinegar
Parmesan cheese, grated
Handful of Italian parsley, chopped

Directions:

Cook the pasta, reserving 1 cup of the pasta cooking water.

Soak dried mushrooms in 1 cup of very hot water for about 20 minutes. Do not discard the soaking liquid. It has lots of flavor and will be added to the pasta. When the mushrooms are soft, chop them.

Slice the fresh mushrooms, or break them up into small pieces, depending on the type of mushroom. Heat butter in a large skillet over medium heat. When butter browns and starts smelling nutty, add the mushrooms. Season with salt and pepper. Sauté the mushrooms until they release their liquid and brown, about 10 to 20 minutes. Lower the heat and add the garlic and the dried mushrooms. Cook just until the garlic becomes fragrant, and then add the sherry vinegar and the soaking liquid from the mushrooms. Be careful not to include the grit that inevitably drifts to the bottom of the soaking liquid.

Add the pasta and, if it looks dry, add some of the pasta cooking water. (I usually add a few splashes, between ¼ and ½ cup until the sauce reaches the desired consistency). Toss everything together, add grated Parmesan cheese and parsley, and serve.

NOTE: Do not skip the parsley! It adds brightness, flavor, and color, and is well worth the chopping time.

Vietnamese Summer Noodles

Serves 4

One of the nice things about this recipe is that it uses rice vermicelli, which cooks by soaking in hot water. On a hot day, I like to eat a light pasta dish without boiling a massive pot of water to cook it. Any rice noodle will work here, or even regular pasta in a pinch. If you are using regular pasta, increase the amount to ¾ of a pound.

Ingredients:

½ pound rice vermicelli
2 tablespoons sugar
4 tablespoons lime juice
2 tablespoons fish sauce
1 teaspoon Sriracha, or other hot sauce, to taste
2 tablespoons rice vinegar
1 carrot, shredded
5 cloves garlic, minced, divided
2 tablespoons vegetable oil

½ pound ground pork
½ pound shrimp, peeled and deveined
Handful of basil leaves, shredded
Handful of cilantro leaves, chopped
Handful of mint leaves, shredded
4 scallions, sliced
1 cup shredded lettuce
1 cucumber, cut into small matchsticks

Directions:

Place vermicelli in a large bowl and pour hot water over the pasta until it is covered. Soak until pasta is pliable, about 5 to 10 minutes, then drain.

Dissolve the sugar in the lime juice in a large bowl. Mix in the fish sauce, the hot sauce, and the rice vinegar. Add the carrot and 1 clove of minced garlic and set aside.

Heat the vegetable oil in a medium pan and sauté the rest of the garlic until it is fragrant, about one minute. Add the pork and cook until it is browned, about 3 to 5 minutes. Add the shrimp, and cook until the shrimp is just pink, another 3 to 5 minutes. Mix the shrimp, pork, and rice vermicelli into the bowl with the sauce. Top with the herbs, scallions, lettuce, and cucumber and serve.

ON FISH SAUCE: Please do not fear the fish sauce! Yes, it smells strange, and the ingredient list is terrifying—it's usually made from fermented anchovy—but fish sauce is one of the keys to making delicious Vietnamese food. It is sold in most grocery stores now, so just buy a bottle and try it. Live dangerously! You won't regret it.

Pasta with Sausage and Mushrooms

Serves 2

Ingredients:

½ pound pasta
1 cup pasta cooking water
About one ounce of dried mixed wild
    mushrooms
1 pint mushrooms
4 cloves garlic

Salt and pepper
½ pound sweet sausage
½ cup white wine
1 small (14-oz) can plum tomatoes
Fresh thyme

Directions:

Cook the pasta, reserving 1 cup of the pasta cooking water.

Put the wild mushrooms in a bowl and pour about ½ cup hot water over them. Let them soak. I like dried porcini mushrooms, but you can use any kind. They generally take about 20 minutes of soaking before they soften up.

Coarsely chop the mushrooms and set aside. Smash and chop the garlic, along with a pinch of salt, until it is a paste. Crumble the sausage into a hot pan and cook, stirring until the sausage browns. Add the mushrooms and the garlic, and cook until the mushrooms release their liquid. Remove the wild mushrooms from the liquid, squeezing them over the bowl, and chop. Add those to the pan, along with the liquid you soaked the mushrooms in. (Sometimes there is grit at the bottom of the mushroom liquid, so be careful not to add that. It won't, needless to say, enhance the dish.) Add the white wine, tomatoes, salt and pepper, and fresh thyme, and simmer for 10 to 15 minutes. If the sauce gets dry, add some of the pasta cooking water.

Toss with cooked pasta and serve.

Pasta Bolognese

Serves 4, with an extra quart of sauce for the freezer

This is a staple in my house. This recipe will make enough sauce for a pound of pasta, with extra to stick in a quart container in the freezer, since it freezes so well. The only hitch is that if you have one pot, you have to make the sauce, then clear everything out of the pot to cook the pasta. I may be the laziest, most dirty-dish averse person on earth, but I still think it's worth the effort.

Ingredients:

1 large onion	Red pepper flakes
2 medium carrots	1½ pounds ground beef
3 celery stalks	1 (4-oz) can tomato paste
3 cloves garlic, minced	1 cup red wine
3 tablespoons olive oil	1 (28-oz) can crushed tomatoes
Salt	1 (14-oz) can chicken stock

Directions:

Finely chop the onion, carrots and celery, and mince the garlic. Heat olive oil in a large pot over medium heat. Add the vegetables, a big pinch of salt, and red pepper flakes to taste, then sauté the vegetables until they are soft, about 10 minutes.

Add the beef, along with another pinch of salt, and brown the beef, breaking it up with a wooden spoon. It will take about 10 minutes to brown the beef. Add the tomato paste and toast it until it is slightly darker in color, about 5 to 8 minutes. Add the wine and stir, letting it reduce. Once the wine has reduced, after about 5 minutes, add the crushed tomatoes and the chicken stock. Stir everything together.

Bring the sauce to a boil and then reduce the heat to low. Let the sauce simmer until it thickens, about 45 minutes. Taste and make sure there is enough salt—it might need more.

Freeze half of the sauce, and toss the rest with your favorite pasta. Don't forget to sprinkle the top with some good Parmesan cheese!

Spaghetti with Corn and Tomatoes

Serves 2, with leftovers

Make this in the late summer, when tomatoes and corn are at their tastiest. I absolutely love the combination of grilled corn and raw tomatoes.

Ingredients:

2 pounds tomatoes	3 cloves garlic
¼ cup olive oil	3 ears corn
Salt and crushed red pepper flakes	1 pound spaghetti
Handful of basil leaves, torn	Grated Parmesan cheese, to taste

Directions:

Put a pot of water up to boil. Coarsely chop the tomatoes and squeeze out the seeds. (Some people might like to peel the tomatoes first. I usually don't bother, but if you prefer skinless tomatoes, drop them in boiling water for 1 minute, and the peel will slide off. You can use the same pot of boiling water that you use to cook the spaghetti.) Put the chopped tomatoes in a large bowl with the olive oil and a generous sprinkling of salt and crushed red pepper flakes. Add the torn basil leaves. Whack the cloves of garlic with the flat of a knife to release their oils, and add them to the bowl. (If you really love garlic, as I do, finely mince one of the cloves and add that as well.)

While the tomatoes are marinating, place the ears of corn on a grill pan, rotating until there are some browned kernels on all sides. (This shouldn't take more than 2–3 minutes per side.) Cut the kernels off the cobs and add to the tomatoes.

Cook the spaghetti until it is al dente. When the spaghetti is ready, remove the whole garlic cloves from the sauce, toss in the pasta, and serve with plenty of Parmesan cheese.

Sesame Noodles

Serves 4 with the chicken, 2 without

For some reason, there are a lot of bad sesame noodles out there. Not only bad tasting noodles, but noodles where the consistency is all wrong. This dish doesn't have that problem. The secret is the water, which helps loosen up the peanut butter and form the tasty sauce. The shredded chicken is optional, but if you do add it, you have a one-dish meal. I like the snow peas in this dish, but you could also shred carrot, or dice peppers, or add any other vegetables you have on hand.

Ingredients:

4 tablespoons soy sauce
3 tablespoons rice vinegar
2 tablespoons toasted sesame oil
1 teaspoon chili oil (optional)
Pinch of salt
Crushed red pepper, to taste
3 tablespoons creamy peanut butter
⅓ cup water (approximate)

2 small cucumbers, like Kirby, or 1 English cucumber
1 cup snow peas
4 scallions
Handful of cilantro
½ pound pasta
2 chicken breasts, cooked and shredded (optional)

Directions:

In the bottom of the bowl in which you intend to serve the noodles, add the soy, rice vinegar, sesame oil, chili oil, salt, and red pepper. Whisk in the peanut butter, and add enough water to get a thin, sauce-like consistency. (I find I usually need about ⅓ cup water.)

Peel the cucumbers and cut into thin matchsticks. Snap the ends off of the snow peas, and pull off any strings, then slice them. Thinly slice the scallions, and chop the cilantro.

Cook the pasta (I use spaghetti). When the pasta is cooked and drained, combine in the bowl with the sauce, using tongs to coat everything. Toss in the vegetables, and the chicken if you are using it, give it another toss, and serve.

NOTE: If you don't like the snow peas raw, you can toss them into the pasta water for the last minute that the pasta cooks, and then drain them with the pasta, to lightly blanch them.

Orzo with Eggplant

Serves 8–10 as a side dish

This is great party food, particularly at things like barbecues. It keeps well and actually tastes better a day or two after you make it. This is the kind of dish you can make on the weekend and then nibble on all week long.

Ingredients:

1 pound of orzo
⅓ cup olive oil, plus oil for the eggplant
1 large eggplant
8–10 sun-dried tomatoes, packed in oil

2 large tomatoes, chopped
2 cloves garlic, chopped
1 red onion, diced
Handful of basil leaves, torn (optional)
3–4 tablespoons balsamic vinegar
Salt and pepper

Directions:
Cook the orzo.

Place a few tablespoons of olive oil in a shallow dish. Slice the eggplant into rounds about ½-inch thick. Using a pastry brush, brush olive oil on both sides of each piece of eggplant, being careful not to use too much—the eggplant will soak up the oil very quickly. Season with salt and broil on each side until brown, about 4 to 5 minutes per side. Let the eggplant cool, then chop it up and put it in a large bowl.

Chop up the sun dried tomatoes, and add them to the bowl, along with some of the oil they were packed in. Dice the tomatoes, chop the garlic, dice the red onion and throw it all into the bowl. Add the basil, if you are using it.

Toss the pasta into the bowl. Add the vinegar, remaining olive oil, and salt and pepper to taste.

ON EGGPLANT: You can broil eggplant the way I described above, toss it with pasta, some of the pasta water, and some good Parmesan cheese and make a meal out of it. Or you can layer the broiled eggplant with store-bought marinara sauce and mozzarella cheese for a quick and easy eggplant parmigiana.

Spaghetti with Asparagus and Mint

Serves 2 with leftovers

This is a light and delicious spring pasta. The asparagus is briefly sautéed with some garlic, and then the spaghetti is tossed in. A mixture of raw garlic, mint, and lemon zest brings flavor and depth, and crumbles of Cotija cheese add a salty component. A squeeze of lemon over the whole works brings everything together. I love using pencil asparagus for this, but any size will do.

Ingredients:

½ pound spaghetti
½ cup fresh mint leaves
3–4 cloves garlic, chopped, divided
1 teaspoon lemon zest
3 tablespoons olive oil, divided

1 large bunch asparagus, cut into bite-sized pieces
Pasta cooking water
½ cup Cotija cheese (or pecorino, or any hard, salty cheese that you like)
Lemon juice, to taste

Directions:

Bring a pot of salted water to a boil and cook the spaghetti until it is al dente. Reserve ½ cup of the pasta cooking water.

Finely chop the mint leaves together with one of the cloves of chopped garlic and the lemon zest, and add a drizzle of olive oil to bring everything together. Season with salt and then set aside.

In a large pan, sauté the rest of the chopped garlic in some olive oil until it is just fragrant, then add the asparagus. Sauté until it is just barely cooked, about 2 to 5 minutes, depending on the thickness of the asparagus. Toss in the spaghetti, together with some of the pasta cooking water. Remove the pan from the heat and add in the mint mixture. Sprinkle the cheese throughout, squeeze some lemon over the top, and serve.

Vegetables and Sides

VEGETABLES AND SIDES: You've got to eat them, so why not make them taste good? Sure, you can always just steam any given vegetable, or pop it into the microwave, but for very little additional effort you can actually enjoy getting your vitamins and minerals. So read on. . . .

Sesame Bok Choy

Serves 2

I love bok choy this way. When it is sautéed quickly, the green leaves wilt but the white stems stay crisp, and it is absolutely delicious. Baby bok choy is best, but any size will do. Toasted sesame oil is not cheap, but it is well worth the investment. A little bit of this oil infuses any dish with a really nice, smoky flavor. It's especially nice with vegetables. Sometimes they sell sesame oil that contains canola oil, but bypass that for the real stuff. You can easily substitute snow peas for bok choy.

Ingredients:

1 pound bok choy
Splash of peanut oil
Red pepper flakes, to taste
Salt, to taste

2 cloves garlic, chopped
2 teaspoons toasted sesame oil
1 tablespoon sesame seeds

Directions:

First, get the bok choy ready. If you are using baby bok choy, you can leave it whole, but with larger sizes of bok choy, simply cut off the ends and cut the leaves in half or thirds. It is better if some of the water from washing the vegetable is still clinging to the leaves.

Heat peanut oil and red pepper flakes in a large pan. When it is hot, throw in the bok choy and season with salt. Wait 2 to 3 minutes, until the green parts of the bok choy begin to wilt. (If the pan looks very dry, you can add a bit of water.) Add the garlic, give it a stir, and cook until the garlic just becomes fragrant, about 1 minute. Add the sesame oil and sesame seeds and serve.

Indian-Style Spinach and Chickpeas

Serves 2

Indian food is one of those cuisines that I love to eat in restaurants but don't usually make at home. This recipe is the exception—it is very easy to make and can be a meal all by itself, with a little rice. Garam masala is a mixture of Indian spices that you can find in most grocery stores

Ingredients:

3 tablespoons olive oil
2 teaspoons cinnamon
1 medium onion, chopped
1 teaspoon salt
6 cloves garlic, chopped
1-inch piece of ginger, grated

2 teaspoons garam masala
1 teaspoon cumin
4–6 plum tomatoes, chopped
1 can chickpeas
1 pound baby spinach, coarsely
    chopped

Directions:

Heat oil over medium heat. Add the cinnamon and wait one minute. Then add the onions, season with salt, and cook until they are soft. Add the garlic and ginger and cook until fragrant, about 1 minute. Add the garam masala and the cumin, again cooking until fragrant, about 1 to 2 minutes. Add the tomatoes and cook until they start to break down, about five minutes. Add the chickpeas and cook until they start to soften, about 5 to 10 minutes. Then add the spinach and cook until the spinach is wilted. Taste and correct the seasoning. Serve over rice.

Sautéed Broccoli

Serves 2

This is really just my version of stir-fry, and you can add any vegetables you want, but broccoli is my favorite, because it catches all that tasty sauce.

Ingredients:

1 tablespoon peanut oil
2 cloves garlic, minced
½ teaspoon red pepper flakes
½ pound broccoli
2 tablespoons soy sauce

1 tablespoon rice wine
1 tablespoon rice vinegar
Splash of water (3–4 tablespoons)
1 tablespoon toasted sesame oil

Directions:

Add the peanut oil, garlic, and pepper flakes to a hot pan. When the garlic is sizzling and fragrant, but before it browns and burns, about one minute, add the broccoli. Give it a toss, and then add the soy sauce, rice wine, rice vinegar, and a splash of water. Sauté until the broccoli is bright green and crisp-tender, add the sesame oil, and serve.

NOTE: You can add any number of vegetables to this dish, or even some chicken, tofu, or shrimp to make a full meal.

Root Vegetable Slaw

Serves 4 as a side dish

You can use whatever root vegetables you like in this dish, or even go crazy and throw in some cabbage. The vegetables are all shredded together, which can be done with a box grater but takes all of 20 seconds if you are lucky enough to have a food processor with a grater attachment. The slaw can literally be assembled in less than 10 minutes, and it improves with age.

Ingredients:

2 tablespoons soy sauce
Hot sauce to taste
2 tablespoons rice vinegar
2 teaspoons toasted sesame oil
4 large radishes
½ small jicama

1 English cucumber (or 2 Kirby cucumbers)
1 small red onion
3 medium carrots
1 inch fresh ginger, peeled
4 scallions
Handful of cilantro

Directions:

In the bottom of a large bowl, mix together the soy sauce, hot sauce, rice vinegar and sesame oil. Grate the radishes, jicama, cucumber, onion, and carrots and add them to the bowl. Finely grate the ginger into the mixture. Slice the scallions, chop the cilantro, and add both to the bowl. Mix well and serve.

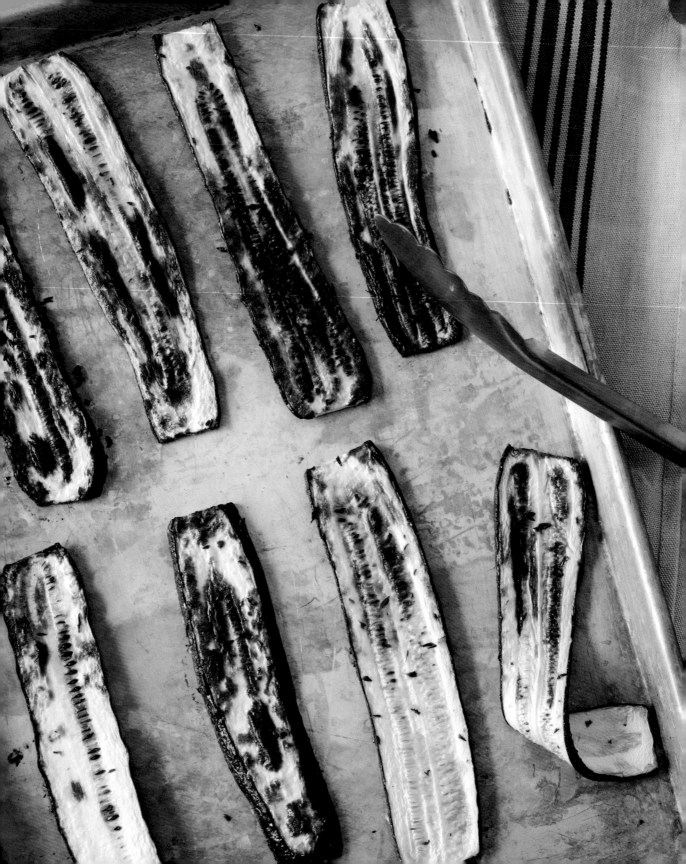

Broiled Zucchini

Serves 2

This is easy, absolutely delicious, and it takes only about 5 minutes to make.

Ingredients:

3 medium zucchini
2 cloves garlic
Big pinch of salt

3 tablespoons olive oil
2 tablespoons fresh thyme

Directions:

Slice each zucchini into long strips, about ¼-inch thick. Smash the cloves of garlic with the side of a knife, sprinkle the garlic with salt, then chop the garlic and salt mixture into a paste.

Put the zucchini and garlic into a plastic bag along with olive oil. Finely chop the fresh thyme and add that to the bag. Seal it and shake the bag around until everything is well mixed.

Turn the broiler on, and cover a cookie sheet in aluminum foil. Lay the zucchini on the cookie sheet. Broil until each side is brown, about 3 to 5 minutes per side, depending on the broiler.

Serve hot or at temperature.

Spinach Pie

Serves 4

I really love spinach pie, and this is a terrific one. I used to be troubled by the Large Volume Spinach Problem: do I buy unwashed spinach, and spend an eternity ridding it of sand? Do I buy roughly a million packages of baby spinach to get the amount of cooked spinach I need? Do I just buy frozen spinach? Since I am lazy, I usually bought frozen spinach but was never quite happy with the results. Then one day I found the answer: organic frozen spinach. It really does make the best spinach pie. (If you don't believe me, conduct a blind taste test with your family and see what they say.)

One last comment: Do not fear the phyllo dough! If you tear some of the phyllo sheets while assembling the pie, just keep going. It won't matter. If you don't want to use phyllo dough, buy frozen puff pastry dough and roll it out to a 12-inch rectangle.

Ingredients:

¼ cup pine nuts
¼ cup olive oil
Red pepper flakes
1 onion, chopped
2 (10-oz) packages of frozen spinach, defrosted and squeezed dry
Salt
2 eggs

½ cup feta cheese
4 tablespoons bread crumbs, divided
3 scallions, thinly sliced
3 tablespoons freshly grated Parmesan cheese
8 sheets of phyllo dough
5 tablespoons unsalted butter
1 tablespoon sesame seeds

Directions:
Preheat oven to 375°F.

In a small dry pan, add the pine nuts and toast them, shaking the pan occasionally and watching the pan carefully, because nuts burn quickly.

In a large pan, heat the olive oil with the red pepper flakes. When the oil is hot, cook the onion until it is soft. Add the spinach, along with a generous pinch of salt, and cook until most of the liquid is gone. Cool the spinach slightly. Meanwhile, in a bowl beat the eggs with the feta cheese, pine nuts, 1 tablespoon of bread crumbs, and the sliced scallions. Mix in the spinach.

Mix together the remainder of bread crumbs with the Parmesan cheese in a small bowl, and melt the butter in another small bowl.

Lay out a sheet of aluminum foil and on that lay the first sheet of phyllo dough. Brush it with butter, and sprinkle with the bread crumb-cheese mixture. Repeat with 7 more sheets of phyllo dough.

Pour the spinach mixture into the middle of the dough, then fold the phyllo dough up around the mixture. There should be a square of spinach in the center, not covered by phyllo dough. Brush butter on the top of the dough, and sprinkle the sesame seeds all over. Bake until it is golden, about 30 minutes. It is delicious warm or at room temperature.

Mashed Cauliflower

Serves 2, with leftovers

Cauliflower is easier to mash than potatoes, and with the addition of cheese it tastes almost as good. I like to use Gruyere cheese, but you can certainly use cheddar, or any other cheese that you like. Try it and see if you can fool your family into thinking they are eating potatoes. . . .

Ingredients:

1 head cauliflower, broken into small florets
¾ cup whole milk
2 tablespoons butter

1 teaspoon paprika
Salt and pepper
¾ cup of shredded cheese

Directions:

Steam the cauliflower until it is soft, about 10 minutes. Transfer the cooked cauliflower to a pot and mash it until it has a relatively smooth consistency. Under low heat, stir in the milk, the butter, and the paprika, and season with salt and pepper. Off the heat, stir in the cheese, and serve hot.

Quinoa with Fried Shallots and Pine Nuts

Serves 4 as a side dish

This is a great way to serve quinoa. The nuttiness of the grain is echoed by the toasted nuts, and all of it plays off of the lemon juice and fruity olive oil. But the star of the dish is really the fried shallots.

Normally, I am opposed to frying at home. I blame Hanukkah for this state of affairs. Every year, I make potato latkes for Hanukkah, and then my apartment smells like burned oil for eleven-and-a-half months, until shortly before the next Hanukkah party. Plus, frying makes a huge mess. But here's the thing: If you thinly slice the shallots and toss them in flour, they will crisp up in a pan with very little oil. The shallots turn golden before the oil can stink up the house. There is no mess, and they are ridiculously tasty.

One more thing: feel free to add any vegetables or cheese to this. I've made the dish with roasted butternut squash, tossed it with fresh greens, and mixed in feta cheese. You can also swap pine nuts for walnuts, or anything you have on hand. But don't omit the shallots; they really make the dish.

Ingredients:

1 cup quinoa
¼ cup pine nuts
Vegetable oil
2–3 shallots

Salt and pepper
2 tablespoons flour
2 tablespoons fresh lemon juice
4 tablespoons best quality olive oil

Directions:

Cook the quinoa according to the instructions on the package. It is cooked like rice, with one part quinoa to two parts water.

While the quinoa is cooking, toast the pine nuts in a dry pan until they are golden. Remove the nuts from the pan, and then heat about ¼ inch of vegetable oil in the same pan. Thinly slice the shallots, and season them with salt and pepper. Dump the flour on a plate, and then coat the shallots in a thin coating of flour and shake off the excess. Fry the shallots until they are crunchy and golden, then put them on paper towels to drain.

In a small bowl, season the lemon juice with salt and pepper, then whisk in olive oil. When the quinoa is cooked, place it in a large bowl and, while it is still hot, mix in olive oil mixture. Sprinkle in the nuts and shallots, and serve.

Roasted Squash (and other vegetables)

Serves 2

I'm almost embarrassed to include this recipe, because it is so easy, but it's a great trick and people love it. Literally, squash is cut into cubes, tossed with olive oil, salt, and pepper, and roasted until brown. You can also spice it up with some cinnamon, cumin, and chili powders.

If you like this dish, try roasting carrots or parsnips the same way.

For parties, I roast a whole mix of vegetables, including carrots, parsnips, zucchini, peppers, onions, and eggplant, and it all tastes wonderful hot or at room temperature. Just increase the olive oil, salt, and pepper to adequately coat the amount of vegetables you roast. Also, it is best to roast the vegetables in a single layer, so if you are roasting a lot of vegetables, use more than one cookie sheet.

Ingredients:

1 large butternut squash
3 tablespoons olive oil

Salt and pepper to taste

Directions:

Preheat the oven to 400°F. Peel the squash, scoop out the seeds, and cut into cubes. Toss the squash on a cookie sheet with olive oil, salt, and pepper. Roast until the squash is golden on the outside, about 40 to 45 minutes.

Brussels Sprout Potato Chips

Serves 2 with leftovers

This is less a recipe than a technique. I love roasted brussels sprouts; they are delicious, any way they are sliced. But if you peel some of the leaves off of the individual sprouts, and roast the leaves and sprouts separately, the leaves become very crispy, almost like potato chips. My kids love them. You can add any flavors you like to this—some chopped pancetta, maybe, or a shot of balsamic vinegar. But I think these are perfect with nothing more than salt, pepper and olive oil.

Ingredients:

1 pound brussels sprouts   Salt and pepper
2 tablespoons olive oil

Directions:
Preheat oven to 375°F.

Wash the brussels sprouts in a bowl of water. Cut the bottom off each sprout, and then cut the sprout in half and peel off some of the leaves, discarding the tough, outermost layer. Once you've halved and peeled leaves off all of the sprouts, spread them on a baking sheet. Toss the sprouts with the olive oil, and season with salt and pepper.

Roast the sprouts until the leaves and brown and crispy, about 20 minutes.

Summer Couscous

Serves 2, with leftovers

Next time you're in the grocery store, please buy some couscous. It's easy to make and really versatile. Couscous is also great hot weather food because it cooks so quickly. Feel free to experiment with the vegetables; try some grated carrot, or even sweeten things up with a handful of raisins.

Ingredients:

1 cup couscous
1 clove garlic, chopped
1 lemon
1 teaspoon cumin
Salt and pepper
3 tablespoons olive oil
2 scallions, thinly sliced

2 small cucumbers, diced
3 tomatoes, seeded and chopped, or
    one pint grape tomatoes, halved
½ red onion, diced
½ cup chickpeas (you can use canned,
    drained and rinsed)
½ cup feta cheese, diced

Directions:

Cook the couscous according to the instructions on the package.

In the bottom of a large, shallow bowl, whisk together the garlic, the juice of the lemon, cumin, salt, pepper, and olive oil. Add all of the chopped vegetables and toss together. Mound the vegetables in the middle of the bowl, then spoon the couscous around the perimeter of the bowl. Top with feta.

Zucchini Pancakes

Serves 4

Another exception to my rule against frying, because these zucchini pancakes are really yummy. I might like them better than potato pancakes—and I looove potato pancakes.

Ingredients:

3–4 medium zucchini
1 egg
1½ teaspoons salt
1 bunch scallions, thinly sliced
1 bunch dill, chopped
¼ cup flour
1 teaspoon baking powder
½ cup feta cheese
3–4 tablespoons vegetable oil

YOGURT SAUCE:
⅔ cup Greek yogurt
1 tablespoons olive oil
1 small clove garlic, smashed and finely chopped
½ teaspoon sumac (optional)
Salt and pepper to taste

Directions:

Grate the zucchini on a box grater, then stick it in a strainer set over a bowl. Mix in the salt, then leave it to drain. Periodically squeeze the liquid out of the zucchini. When it is finished, the zucchini should be pretty dry and the volume of zucchini should have reduced considerably. You'll wind up with about 1½ cups of zucchini.

Mix the zucchini with the egg, scallions, dill, flour, baking powder and feta cheese.

In a small bowl, mix together the yogurt, garlic, olive oil, and sumac. Add salt and pepper to taste, and set aside.

Heat the vegetable oil over medium high heat. Drop large spoons of zucchini batter into the pan, and fry until both sides are crisp and brown. Serve with yogurt sauce.

Foolproof Desserts

DESSERTS: I have a confession to make. I can't really bake. I hate to measure, and sifting is something that is just not in my vocabulary. So the recipes in this chapter are, trust me, idiot-proof. These are my stand-by desserts, for the occasions when I think a store-bought dessert just won't cut it. So all of you non-bakers out there, give these a try.

Fruit-Topped Cake

Makes one 9-inch cake

This is my mom's recipe, and it is the easiest, most versatile and tastiest dessert I know. If you are a baking novice, try this cake. It's really, really hard to screw up.

Ingredients:

1 cup sugar
½ cup butter
1 cup flour (supposedly sifted, but I never do)
1 teaspoon baking powder
Pinch of salt
2 eggs

2–3 cups of the fruit of your choice, sliced (apples, pears, peaches and nectarines, or some combination, all work well)
1 lemon
Cinnamon
Sugar
¼ cup apricot preserves

Directions:

Preheat the oven to 350°F. Cream the sugar together with the butter, beating until, well, creamy and pale. Add the flour, baking powder, and salt. Mix in the eggs, and then spread the cake in the bottom of a 9-inch springform pan.

After you slice the fruit, toss with the juice of one lemon to preserve the color. Place the sliced fruit in concentric circles on top of the cake. Sprinkle with cinnamon and sugar.

Bake at 350°F for one hour. After the cake has cooled, spread melted apricot preserves on top.

Rugelach

Makes 4 dozen cookies

This was my great-grandmother's recipe. Rugelach are, concededly, a pain in the neck to make, but the result is worth the effort. They also freeze really well.

Ingredients:

2 sticks butter
½ pound cream cheese
2 cups flour
1 teaspoon cinnamon
1 cup sugar

½ cup chopped walnuts
½ cup raisins
Seedless raspberry or apricot jelly or ½
    cup good quality chocolate chips

Directions:

Preheat the oven to 375°F. Blend the butter, cream cheese, and flour together. Divide the dough into four balls, flatten each ball, and refrigerate until chilled.

Mix together the cinnamon and sugar. Sprinkle a work surface with some of the cinnamon sugar (much as you would flour a surface before rolling out dough). Roll out a ball of the dough, using the cinnamon-sugar as you would use flour, to prevent the dough from sticking, until it is about ¼-inch thick and a 12-inch circle. Spread a thin layer of jelly on top, then sprinkle with nuts and raisins. Alternatively, simply sprinkle with nuts, raisins, and chocolate chips. Cut the circle into 12 wedges. Roll each wedge up, rolling from the outside toward the center, and place the cookies on a cookie sheet that has a Silpat on it. Sprinkle some cinnamon sugar over the top of the cookies.

Bake at 375°F for about 20 minutes.

NOTE ON BAKING: If you put too much jelly on the cookie, it will ooze out and burn all over the cookie sheet. This can be totally avoided by baking the cookies on a Silpat. If you don't have a Silpat and don't feel like shelling out the roughly $20 to buy one, you can also line the cookie sheet with parchment paper. Otherwise, be prepared to sacrifice some of your cookies.

Bread Pudding

Makes one 9×13-inch pudding

I like this recipe because nothing needs to be measured exactly and it always winds up tasting delicious. This is a basic bread pudding recipe, and you can easily add all kinds of different flavors, like chocolate, pumpkin, apple, pecan or anything else you can think of. Serve warm.

Ingredients:

½ cup (1 stick) butter
½ cup sugar
½ cup brown sugar
3 eggs
1½ cups whole milk
1½ cups heavy cream

2 teaspoons vanilla
1 teaspoon cinnamon
½ teaspoon nutmeg
6 cups Challah or Brioche bread, torn
    into pieces
½ cup raisins

Directions:

Preheat the oven to 350°F. Beat together the butter and both kinds of sugar. Beat in the eggs, then stir in the milk, cream, vanilla, cinnamon, and nutmeg. Add the bread and raisins and stir until it looks saturated. Pour into a greased lasagna pan or casserole dish big enough to hold the entire pudding. Bake for 1½ hours.

Brown Butter Sea Salt Chocolate Chip Cookies

Makes about 2 dozen cookies

Warning: These cookies are addictive. It might seem annoying to have to brown the stick of butter, and then cool before adding it to the cookie dough, but what you gain in flavor makes it all worthwhile. The whole wheat flour is optional, but I think it adds a nice nutty undertone. The only problem with these cookies is that there are never enough of them; they always disappear in record time.

Ingredients:

2 sticks of unsalted butter, softened, divided
1 cup brown sugar
½ cup white sugar
2 teaspoons vanilla extract
2 eggs
1¾ cups all-purpose flour
½ cup whole wheat flour (you can replace with all-purpose flour if you wish)
1 teaspoon salt
1 teaspoon baking soda
1½ cups chocolate chips
Sea salt, for sprinkling

Directions:

Brown 1 stick of butter in a saucepan over medium low heat. Once the butter is brown and smells nutty, allow it to cool. (You can put it in the refrigerator to speed up this process.)

In a large bowl, cream together the other stick of butter, together with the brown sugar and white sugar. Mix until light and fluffy. Add the vanilla, and mix for another minute. Slowly add the cooled brown butter, and mix for a couple of minutes. Mix in the eggs until they are fully incorporated.

In a medium bowl, mix together the flours, salt, and baking soda. (You're supposed to sift the dry ingredients, but I never do.) Add the dry mixture to the butter mixture, and stir together until the flour is just incorporated.

Fold in the chocolate chips. Cover and chill the dough in the refrigerator for at least 30 minutes.

Once the dough is chilled, preheat the oven to 350°F. Use a tablespoon to scoop out cookies, and place the about 2 inches apart on a cookie sheet. Press each cookie down slightly, then sprinkle with sea salt.

Bake for 10 to 12 minutes, or until they are golden brown.

Fruit Crumble

Makes one 9×13-inch crumble

You can serve this over any fruit that is in season. This is another dessert I rely on because no sifting is required, and all amounts are approximate—in other words, you really can't screw this one up. Literally all you need to do is mix together the topping, cut up some fruit, dump it in a dish with lemon juice and sugar, cover with the topping, and bake. It's terrific with some vanilla ice cream.

Ingredients:

2 pounds apples, pears, berries, stone
   fruit or some combination
1 teaspoon lemon zest (you can also
   use orange zest)
2 tablespoons sugar
1 tablespoon flour
1 tablespoon lemon juice (you can also
   use orange juice)

CRUMBLE TOPPING:
¾ cup flour
½ cup oats
½ cup light brown sugar, packed
6 tablespoons butter, melted
1 tablespoon cinnamon
½ teaspoon nutmeg
Big pinch of salt

Directions:

Preheat oven to 350°F. Mix all of the crumble ingredients until they are in clumps. Set aside.

Cut whatever fruit you are using into uniform pieces. Dump the fruit into a large bowl and zest the lemon over the top. Add the sugar, flour, and lemon juice. Taste the fruit, and if it is very sour you might want to sprinkle a bit more sugar.

Pour the fruit mixture into a large casserole dish and spread the crumble mixture evenly over the top. Bake until the fruit is bubbling and the topping is crunchy, about 30 to 40 minutes.

Buttermilk Coffee Cake

Makes one 9-inch round cake

I come from a family of coffeecake lovers. Several of my family members are indifferent to chocolate (a gene that bypassed me entirely) but are helpless before a crumb topping. So, I've long sought the perfect coffeecake, something consistently tasty and made with a minimum of fuss. As it turns out, the key is buttermilk. This cake has a generous amount of the magic ingredient, and it always results in a light, moist, delicious cake, without the tedium of sifting or the frustration of trying to bring an egg to room temperature. Best of all, you don't even need to get out the mixer.

Ingredients:

½ cup pecans
2 cups of all-purpose flour + 1 tablespoon
   flour for the pan
1 cup sugar
1 teaspoon salt
1 stick butter, room temperature + 3
   tablespoons butter, divided
1 teaspoon baking powder

½ teaspoon baking soda
¾ cup buttermilk
2 teaspoons vanilla
1 egg
1 tablespoon lemon zest
⅔ cup brown sugar
2 teaspoons cinnamon

Directions:

Preheat oven to 350°F. Butter a 9-inch springform pan, then dust it with the extra tablespoon of flour.

In a dry pan, toast the pecans until they are fragrant. If they are whole, coarsely chop them. (I do this by putting them in a bag and whacking the bag with a rolling pin.). Set the chopped pecans aside.

Put flour, sugar, and salt in a bowl. Add the softened stick of butter, cut up, and rub the mixture into the flour until it resembles coarse meal. (I use my fingers.) Remove 1 cup of this mixture and set it aside—it will become the base for the crumb topping.

Add baking powder, baking soda, buttermilk, vanilla, egg, and lemon zest to the flour mixture, and mix with a wooden spoon until it is combined. Pour it into the springform pan.

Add the pecans to the leftover cup of the flour mixture, together with the brown sugar and cinnamon. Melt the remaining 3 tablespoons of butter and add it to the mixture, combining until it is coarse crumbs. Spread the crumb mixture evenly over the top of the cake.

Bake until it is done, about 45 minutes. Cool completely and serve.

Pound Cake Filled with Berries

Makes 1 loaf

This is one of my sister's go-to desserts. It looks beautiful and tastes delicious; the sour cream keeps the cake really moist.

Ingredients:

½ cup unsalted butter at room temperature, plus more to grease the pan

1¼ cups sugar

1 tablespoon grated lemon zest, divided

3 eggs

1 teaspoon vanilla

2 cups flour (plus extra for the pan)

½ teaspoon baking soda

1 teaspoon baking powder

½ teaspoon salt

¾ cup sour cream

1½ cups fresh raspberries or blackberries, or a combination

A little powdered sugar (optional)

Directions:

Preheat oven to 350°F. Butter and flour an 8.5×4.5×2.5-inch loaf pan.

Put the butter in the microwave for 10 seconds to soften it up, then mix it with the sugar until light and fluffy. (You can do this with an electric mixer or a wooden spoon.) Mix in half the lemon zest. Add the eggs and mix until light and fluffy, then add the vanilla.

In another bowl, mix the flour, baking soda, baking powder, and salt. Add a little of this to the wet ingredients then add some of the sour cream and mix. Continue alternating adding dry ingredients and sour cream until both are fully mixed in with the wet ingredients.

Wash and dry the berries, then gently mix them with the remainder of the lemon zest. You can add more lemon zest to taste, especially if the berries are very sweet.

Spread about half the batter (or a little less) into the loaf pan, then add the berries on top, leaving a rim of batter surrounding the berries. You might not fit all the berries. Then add the remainder of the batter on top.

Bake about an hour, until a toothpick comes out clean.

Dust with powdered sugar if you want. It's great served with vanilla ice cream or fruit sorbet.

Cranberry Pistachio Cookies

Makes about 2 dozen cookies

This is a gem of a recipe from *Gourmet* magazine. It's the perfect dessert recipe, because the cookies look fancy, taste delicious, and they are really easy to make.

Ingredients:

1½ sticks of unsalted butter, softened
⅓ cup sugar
1 teaspoon freshly grated orange rind
1½ cups flour
½ teaspoon cinnamon
¼ teaspoon salt

½ cup dried cranberries
½ shelled pistachios, coarsely chopped
　(don't use the red ones)
1 egg, beaten
¼ cup coarse sugar

Directions:

If the butter is not soft, an easy way to soften it is by zapping it in a microwave for just 10 or 12 seconds.

Using an electric mixer, beat together the sugar, orange rind, and softened butter in a bowl until it is light and fluffy. Mix in the flour, cinnamon, and salt. Stir in the cranberries and pistachios until they are just combined. Gather the dough together, then divide it into two equal pieces, and roll each piece into a log about 2 inches in diameter. Wrap each log in plastic wrap and chill until they are very firm, at least an hour.

Preheat oven to 350°F. Brush beaten egg along the sides of the logs, then roll each log of cookie dough in coarse sugar, until it is pretty evenly covered. Alternatively, you can sprinkle the coarse sugar around each log until it is covered.

Cut each log into ¼-inch-thick slices, then place the slices on a cookie sheet and bake until they are gold around the edges, about 15 to 18 minutes.

About the Author & Photographer

Hope Korenstein loves food so she learned how to cook. She is an attorney by day and an intrepid home cook by night. She lives in Brooklyn with her two children.

Photo credit: Joseph Merlone

Jennifer Silverberg is a food photographer and director, and a visual storyteller for brands and magazines. She was recently named one of the 200 Best Advertising Photographers in the world by Lürzer's Archive. When not behind the lens, she can generally be found enjoying the kitchen in her newly built studio, cooking up feasts for family and friends alike. Honestly . . . anyone who stops by the space, who might be even a little hungry, is welcome to join the festivities. Jennifer, a New York native, now makes her home in St. Louis, Missouri.

Inspiration

How I Escape "The Dinner Rut"

There are a lot of disadvantages to having a small kitchen, but there is one big advantage: That small kitchen is usually in a big city, which is full of really great food, and not just at four-star restaurants. I am lucky enough to live and work in New York City, a place that is filled with taco trucks, falafel stands, noodle joints, dumpling shops, pizza places, and sandwiches from banh mi to tortas. When I fall into a dinner rut, and I'm in need of some inspiration, I invariably find something new and different to sample. That gets me thinking about how to incorporate some of those new flavors into the dinners I cook, often with great results.

I also try to break out of the dinner rut at the grocery store, or, ideally, the farmer's market. If I see weird vegetables in the produce aisle that I've never noticed before, I'll take the plunge and buy them. If I can't find someone at the market who knows about the aforementioned weird vegetables, I usually go online and get information at http://www.epicurious.com.

Above all, I love to try new things. For every new food that tastes like dirty socks, there is something so delicious and amazing that I want to eat it over and over again.

Conversion Charts

METRIC AND IMPERIAL CONVERSIONS
(These conversions are rounded for convenience)

Ingredient	Cups/Tablespoons/ Teaspoons	Ounces	Grams/Milliliters
Butter	1 cup/ 16 tablespoons/ 2 sticks	8 ounces	230 grams
Cheese, shredded	1 cup	4 ounces	110 grams
Cream cheese	1 tablespoon	0.5 ounce	14.5 grams
Cornstarch	1 tablespoon	0.3 ounce	8 grams
Flour, all-purpose	1 cup/1 tablespoon	4.5 ounces/0.3 ounce	125 grams/8 grams
Flour, whole wheat	1 cup	4 ounces	120 grams
Fruit, dried	1 cup	4 ounces	120 grams
Fruits or veggies, chopped	1 cup	5 to 7 ounces	145 to 200 grams
Fruits or veggies, pureed	1 cup	8.5 ounces	245 grams
Honey, maple syrup, or corn syrup	1 tablespoon	0.75 ounce	20 grams
Liquids: cream, milk, water, or juice	1 cup	8 fluid ounces	240 milliliters
Oats	1 cup	5.5 ounces	150 grams
Salt	1 teaspoon	0.2 ounce	6 grams
Spices: cinnamon, cloves, ginger, or nutmeg (ground)	1 teaspoon	0.2 ounce	5 milliliters
Sugar, brown, firmly packed	1 cup	7 ounces	200 grams
Sugar, white	1 cup/1 tablespoon	7 ounces/0.5 ounce	200 grams/12.5 grams
Vanilla extract	1 teaspoon	0.2 ounce	4 grams

OVEN TEMPERATURES

Fahrenheit	Celsius	Gas Mark
225°	110°	¼
250°	120°	½
275°	140°	1
300°	150°	2
325°	160°	3
350°	180°	4
375°	190°	5
400°	200°	6
425°	220°	7
450°	230°	8

Index